EDUCATION WITHOUT SCHOOLS

EDUCATION WITHOUT SCHOOLS

edited by

PETER BUCKMAN

with contributions from

Ivan Illich
Ian Lister
Ken Coates
Colin Ward
Michael Armstrong
Michael Macdonald-Ross
Alison Truefitt & Peter Newell
John Hipkin
Albert Hunt
Brian Winston
Richard Rowson
Joe Ravetz

A CONDOR BOOK
SOUVENIR PRESS (EDUCATIONAL & ACADEMIC) LTD.

First published 1973 by
Souvenir Press (Educational & Academic) Ltd.,
95 Mortimer Street, London, W.1

ISBN 0 285 64721 0 paperback
ISBN 0 285 64720 2 casebound

Made and printed in Great Britain by
Willmer Brothers Limited, Birkenhead

Contents

PETER BUCKMAN

Editorial Introduction

Education is not schooling. Schools that are tied to curricula, exams, grades and certificates; schools that rely on compulsory attendance, and expend more energy on a custodial role than an educative one; schools that are licensed by the state to wield a monopoly of 'certifiable knowledge' – these institutions *prevent* a pupil from knowing enough about the workings of society to enable her or him to understand and change it. Such schooling is merely a process of blatant social engineering.

By education I mean a process of understanding the world, of acquiring the confidence to explore its workings. It is, of course, an essential part of maturity. Thomas Jefferson and John Dewey looked on universal education as a means of equipping men to discover their beliefs and to create their institutions; the Brazilian Paulo Freire has described it as a process of becoming critically aware of one's reality in a manner which leads to effective action upon it.

All that, however, is theory. What I imagine most people to want from education is the chance to develop and enlarge their interests so that they may play a more effective part in their society. This does not mean starting a revolution: for most, it means earning more money, the present key to social power. Most people would like to acquire this education in a context that stimulated their imaginations and brought them into contact with people of like interests and with experts worthy of respect. This is how groups work that are dedicated to pursuits such as photography or steam-trains.

But schooling does not meet these requirements. A school is now a place where pupils are forced by law to attend for most of their youth; where the teacher – who is but the servant of the system – rather than the pupil decides what is learnt, when and how it is learnt, and what is considered 'proficiency' in the subject; and where people of differing origins and beliefs are moulded into a common conception of society. No adult would

1

willingly accept such limitations on personal freedom once she or he had escaped school.

The school does indeed hold some of the keys to a better future for those that stay its course, because of the monopoly it holds over the distribution of 'knowledge'. A society that decides that the best jobs should go to those with the largest number of certificates (regardless of the relevance of those certificates to the jobs available), and which gives the granting of such certificates exclusively to the schools, would be considered totalitarian or (worse) inefficient and corrupt, if it licensed similar monopolies in the commercial field. Yet all the world's societies, with the exception of a few isolated tribes, enforce such monopolies over the minds of their children, through their schools.

It is the contention of the contributors to this book that institutionalized schooling cannot provide the education we may demand if we are to gain a greater understanding of our society, and exercise a more effective role in it. All of us share the view that compulsory schooling actually stands in the way of education in its wider sense – that, indeed, given its hierarchical and institutional nature, it cannot do otherwise. But the purpose of this collection is not merely to make out the case against schools, which has so often been done. It is to present, in a detailed and practical manner, ways in which education without schools might and does work – an education that meets the demands of people of all ages, living under the present social system. These ways do not depend on a utopian future, or communities of isolated fanatics, or on renouncing the ways of the world. Still less do they depend on a sudden blinding revelation on the part of those who manage our society. Schools will be with us for some time to come: each of these essays, by combining radicalism with practicality, is rooted in the present while being a pointer to the future.

It is the easiest thing in the world to declare a crisis in education : the condition is practically endemic. But when education is taken to mean schooling, which in turn is a microcosm of the society it serves, in talking of crisis we mean a crisis in society at large. That we are in such a crisis (as so often before), few would deny, even if it is taken to be merely a crisis of con-

2

fidence. Whatever happens, both schooling and education must be affected. The most radical critics know that the realization of their dreams depends on a social revolution. The most conservative accept that things must either go backwards or forwards: they cannot stand still. Left and Right meet around such bemusing themes as vouchers for lifelong education. Those who attack schooling are in turn attacked by professional educators with impeccably liberal credentials. The deschoolers – those who want to abolish compulsory schooling and the monopoly of 'knowledge' by educational institutions – are accused of ushering in a new Dark Age.

But consider the situation. Violence, truancy, and dissatisfaction with school are widely publicized, though they are probably no more significant than they have ever been. What counts is that more and more people inside and outside the schools are aware that the institutions are not living up to their promises; and moreover that society cannot for long afford the cost of financing schooling the way it does now.

Then there is the new and critical factor of adult 'leisure', or what used to be called unemployment. The number of schoolleavers unable to get jobs is already high – highest for those who dropped out earliest. But the peculiar economic pattern of rising adult unemployment combined with inflation in the advanced countries presents a new problem to the managers of the system: what to do with those for whom there is no work, and little possibility of getting any.

This situation, which is aggravating daily, is going to call for social management on a larger scale than ever before – or, as some optimists profess to believe, it will soon lead to the total collapse of the system. Assuming that the latter is unlikely, solutions that seem possible are a shorter working week, greater use of shift-work, each shift being shorter than at present, longer holidays, and earlier retirement on bigger pensions. It is expected that leisure industries will expand, along with service industries. But if the traditional pattern of working is to change – which it must – this will involve new concepts in education. Firstly, working people will have to get used to the idea of changing their occupations several times during their lifetime. This invalidates the argument that the school-based curriculum is efficiently geared to the needs of business: it is too inflexible to cope

3

with an even more changeable demand for training than at present. Secondly, 'leisured' persons, unless they are to watch television twenty-four hours a day (which is possible, except that they'd need to escape from the house for some period daily: perhaps the cinemas will make a comeback after all), will want, or even demand, the opportunity to develop existing or new interests, partly as a hobby, partly to train for different occupations. This demand for education will not be met by schools as they are presently organized: no adult would stand for them.

On the one hand, then, our current crisis affects the schools which hold our children. On the other, it affects the whole pattern of social life. Nor should anyone imagine that massive social engineering is impossible short of 1984: the ever more widely publicized calls for controls on the abuse of our environment, if we are to avoid a dead world, evidence a wish at all levels (from the Common Market's Council of Rome to the Friends of the Earth) for more and better management. Short of total chaos, indeed, it is suggested that this is the only solution.

If a violently different pattern of social life were soon to come into being, where would this leave the schools? Too much investment, historical and financial, has gone into them to allow them to be scrapped overnight. Yet this investment, which is rising exponentially, must soon be exhausted, unless state spending priorities are dramatically altered: the money isn't there to continue. That is one reason why the schools cannot meet their promise to provide equality of opportunity for every pupil. The splendid idea of education (meaning schooling) as the great leveller has never had a basis in truth, now or in the past. Not only do the capitalist countries lavish a far greater proportion of their educational budgets on the children of the privileged rather than those of the deprived, but institutional schooling, by its very nature, conditions its pupils to accept a social system that is very far from egalitarian. The marvellous primary schools that encourage initiative, curiosity, and creativity in their kids, for which parts of England are famous, are tolerated because all that will be knocked out of the kids by their secondary schools, with their timetables, curricula, and grades. It is of course true – and a fact that must be celebrated – that school has given many children from deprived homes the chance

4

of betterment. But by faithfully reflecting the hierarchical and unequal structure of the society it serves, school perpetuates the social barriers the deprived seek to cross.

Ivan Illich argues in his essay that the solution is to abolish compulsory schooling altogether, and to devote the vast funds thereby released to a true education for every citizen that would last from cradle to grave. (One silliness about confusing education with schooling is the notion that, for most kids, their 'education' is over and done with by the age of sixteen, or whatever the school-leaving age is.) Ken Coates writes of the close links between education and industry, and argues that for education to be a lifelong experience, control by working people over their working lives is essential. When we talk – as we are in this book – of education embracing everything and everybody, regardless of age or station, we should know that there are various ways in which this education can be realized, without either relying on the schools, or awaiting their abolition.

We learn most from our surroundings, from our friends, and from people who share our interests, in groups: John Hipkin analyses the dynamics of group learning and outlines ways in which they can be used to tackle specific tasks. Improvisation, as Albert Hunt points out, is a learning technique that has had startling results in communities, schools, and drama groups: as a learning tool it has radical applications that anyone can employ.

Many thousands of post-school adults pursue their interests in adult education institutes, which resemble the best of the primary schools in that the courses are oriented towards the pupil rather than the teacher, multiple choices are offered, and, for the most part, there is no grading or examination of results. The Open University, the establishment of which the British Labour leader Harold Wilson regards as his finest achievement, is of course similar to school in that it is institutionalized, sticks rigidly to its curricula, and grades its pupils. Nevertheless it is voluntary, and the substantial response it has had from applicants points to the possibilities of learning, without compulsion, for learning's sake. Richard Rowson discusses the motivation for such learning, stressing the need for a tutorial relationship based on mutual respect rather one-way communication, from teacher to pupil.

The Open University relies on television, radio, and books, the classic media for self-help in education. Brian Winston demonstrates the limitations of the existing media in bringing about that radical change in education that is so often promised. If literacy is the key to written self-expression, fluency in handling technical equipment is the key to self-expression in terms of visual technology: Winston writes of the use of equipment that would make this self-expression universally possible. (Albert Hunt, too, has had experience with kids he has encouraged to use such equipment.) While literacy can never lose its importance as the basis of human communication, even in those societies that emphasize visuals, reading seems to be losing its lustre as a useful skill (a fact which I as a writer deplore). Rarely heard amongst the clamorous arguments over the growing number of illiterates that emerge from our schools is the question 'What is reading being taught *for*?' The written word, in books and papers, undoubtedly remains the most effective medium for close argument, but perhaps for a minority – and moreover a minority which, however privileged at the moment, might find its ignorance of technology consigning it too to early retirement. For me the argument about the teaching of reading centres on social priorities rather than learning methods: why should kids bother to acquire a skill that is useless or irrelevant to them? Reading is not, and rarely has been, the key to social advantage, even when society did its business in letters rather than numbers or images. Class barriers were not crossed by the few because of their reading skill, but because of their ability to use that skill to manipulate the levers of society. Those levers no longer seem to depend on literacy: its revival and importance will depend on a culture which values, and does not debase, self-expression in speech and writing. Paulo Freire in Brazil, and others in North American ghettoes, discovered that illiterates rapidly learnt to read when the words they were interested in were relevant to their social and political situation. The rising number of illiterates in today's schools are less victims of bad teaching than prisoners in a culture where reading above a basic level is sadly irrelevant to them. To change this course requires people fluent in reading and enthusiastic about its social, political, and cultural possibilities. These are, unfortunately, allowed little scope inside schools.

Any kind of education depends on a relationship between the learner and the person she or he learns from. Learning is not, of course, the same as teaching: the latter is too often an exercise in management, in getting the pupil round to the teacher's point of view. Michael Armstrong argues in his essay that the true role of the teacher should be to encourage learning as a sustained, communal, and above all collaborative exercise, between people who know and respect each other as well as their subject. Education also depends on skills useful to the learner, both as a matter of personal survival, and in a society that will emphasize job-mobility. The testing of such skills should depend on the ability of the subject to perform the task set, not on the regurgitation of what has been learnt in a manner that will please the examiner. Michael Macdonald-Ross discusses, from the point of view of an educational technologist, how skills can be (and already are) acquired and tested without relying on the monopoly over certification the schools currently enjoy. That monopoly is bolstered by the exam-curriculum system: Alison Truefitt and Peter Newell write of the false arguments underpinning school reliance on it, and the dangers inherent in its burgeoning commercial exploitation.

The argument of the deschooler is that compulsory schooling should be abolished. This is most unlikely in the near future. The most common objections offered to deschooling by those who criticise the current system are that, without compulsion, kids from deprived homes would never get the change to better themselves, that they would be open to exploitation, get into mischief, and, worst, grow up in invincible ignorance. The answer of the deschooler is that compulsion cannot work in any circumstances, that the risks of doing away with it are worth running, that people learn what they need to know outside rather than inside the schools, and that children in schools anyway grow up ignorant of the things that matter to them because of the very nature of the institutions. It matters little they say, whether the school is hidebound or a Free School: the nature of the beast cannot be changed.

The objectors are not satisfied with these arguments. But as both Ian Lister and Colin Ward make clear in their contribu-

7

tions, however unlikely the imminent abolition of schools, the analysis of people like Illich remains valid. We are writing of a fluid situation containing several possibilities for change, but we cannot escape the present or wish it away. The state, for example, will obviously continue to be the dominant factor in education, with or without schools: Colin Ward discusses how its interference can be minimized. Ian Lister writes of arriving at education without schools from the situation in which we find ourselves: though they might be considered merely 'reformist', the many experiments in deinstitutionalized education (as far as such a thing is possible) provide useful guides to a viable future.

The emphasis of this book is on education as a lifelong experience. It would not be complete without the contribution of Joe Ravetz, on learning from a pupil's point of view. An English teenager, Ravetz is in the rare position of having opted out of school as a matter of personal choice in order to pursue his education on his own. Far from being a dropout, he believes in the principle of education as a liberating tool as firmly as any theorist. Whilst 'education' is synonymous with schooling and remains in the hands of duly certified teachers, and whilst certification remains the sole key to employment – which it cannot for long, whatever happens – the more advanced proposals of those who want to abolish compulsory schooling will remain academic. But Joe Ravetz chose to abandon the system while perforce observing its precepts. His essay outlines the drawbacks and possibilities of so doing. It rounds off a book whose practical aim is to restore education to the hands and minds of everyone who wants it.

IVAN ILLICH

The Deschooled Society

For generations we have tried to make the world a better place by providing more and more schooling, but so far the endeavor has failed. What we have learned instead is that forcing all children to climb an open-ended education ladder cannot enhance equality but must favour the individual who starts out earlier, healthier, or better prepared; that enforced instruction deadens for most people the will for independent learning; and that knowledge treated as a commodity, delivered in packages, and accepted as private property once it is acquired, must always be scarce.

I believe that the disestablishment of the school has become inevitable and that this end of an illusion should fill us with hope. But I also believe that the end of the 'age of schooling' could usher in the epoch of the global schoolhouse that would be distinguishable only in name from a global madhouse or global prison in which education, correction, and adjustment become synonymous. I therefore believe that the breakdown of the school forces us to look beyond its imminent demise and to face fundamental alternatives in education. Either we can work for fearsome and new educational devices that teach about a world which progressively becomes more opaque and forbidding for man, or we can set the conditions for a new era in which technology would be used to make society more simple and transparent, so that all men can once again know the facts and use the tools that shape their lives. In short, we can disestablish schools or we can deschool culture.

The Hidden Curriculum of Schools
In order to see clearly the alternatives we face, we must first distinguish learning from schooling, which means separating the humanistic goal of the teacher from the impact of the invariant structure of the school. This hidden structure constitutes a course of instruction that stays forever beyond the control of the

9

teacher or of his school board. It conveys indelibly the message that only through schooling can an individual prepare himself for adulthood in society, that what is not taught in school is of little value, and that what is learned outside of school is not worth knowing. I call it the hidden curriculum of schooling because it constitutes the unalterable framework of the system, within which all changes in the curriculum are made.

The hidden curriculum is always the same regardless of school or place. It requires all children of a certain age to assemble in groups of about thirty, under the authority of a certified teacher, for some 500 or 1000 or more hours per year. It does not matter whether the curriculum is designed to teach the principles of Fascism, liberalism, Catholicism, socialism, or liberation, so long as the institution claims the authority to define which activities are legitimate 'education'. It does not matter whether the purpose of the school is to produce Soviet or United States citizens, mechanics, or doctors, as long as you can not be a legitimate citizen or doctor *unless* you are a graduate. It makes no difference whether all meetings occur in the same place so long as they are somehow understood as attendance: cane-cutting is work for cane-cutters, correction for prisoners, and part of the curriculum for students.

What is important in the hidden curriculum is that students learn that education is valuable when it is acquired in the school through a gradual process of consumption; that the degree of success the individual will enjoy in society depends on the amount of learning he consumes; and that learning *about* the world is more valuable than learning *from* the world. The imposition of *this* hidden curriculum within an educational programme distinguishes schooling from other forms of planned education. All the world's school systems have common characteristics in relation to their institutional output, and these are the result of the common hidden curriculum of all schools.

Educational reformers who accept the idea that schools have failed fall into three groups. The most respectable are certainly the great masters of alchemy who promise better schools — alchemists being those who sought to refine base elements by leading their distilled spirits through twelve stages of successive enlightenment, so that for their own good and for all the world's benefit they might be transmuted into gold. The most

10

seductive reformers are those popular magicians who promise to make every kitchen into an alchemic lab. The most sinister are the new Masons of the Universe who want to transform the entire world into one huge temple of learning.

Notable among today's masters of alchemy are certain research directors employed or sponsored by the large foundations who believe that schools, if they could somehow be improved, could also become economically more feasible than those that are now in trouble, and simultaneously could sell a larger package of services. Those who are concerned mainly with the curriculum claim that it is outdated or irrelevant. So the curriculum is filled with new packaged courses on African Culture, North American Imperialism, Women's Lib, Pollution, or the Consumer Society. Passive learning is wrong – it is indeed – so we graciously allow students to decide what and how they want to be taught. School are prison houses. Therefore principals are authorized to approve teach-outs, moving the school desks to a roped-off Harlem street. Sensitivity training becomes fashionable. So we import group therapy into the classroom. School, which was supposed to teach everybody everything, now becomes all things to all children.

Other critics emphasize that schools make inefficient use of modern science. Some would administer drugs to make it easier for the instructor to change the child's behaviour. Others would transform school into a stadium for educational gaming. Still others would electrify the classroom. If they are simplistic disciples of McLuhan, they replace blackboards and textbooks with multimedia happenings; if they follow Skinner, they claim to be able to modify behaviour more efficiently than old-fashioned classroom practitioners can.

Most of these changes have, of course, some good effects. The experimental schools have fewer truants. Parents do have a greater feeling of participation in a decentralized district. Pupils, assigned by their teacher to an apprenticeship, do often turn out more competent than those who stay in the classroom. Some children do improve their knowledge of Spanish in the language lab because they prefer playing with the knobs of a tape recorder to conversation with their Puerto Rican peers. Yet all these improvements operate within predictably narrow limits, since they leave the hidden curriculum of school intact. Some reformers would like to shake loose from the hidden curriculum of public schools, but they rarely succeed. Free schools that lead to further free schools produce a mirage of freedom, even though the chain of attendance is often interrupted by long stretches of loafing. Attendance through seduction inculcates the need for educational treatment more persuasively than the reluctant attendance enforced by a truant officer. Permissive teachers in a padded classroom can easily render their pupils impotent to survive once they leave.

Learning in these schools often remains nothing more than the acquisition of socially valued skills defined, in this instance, by the consensus of a commune rather than by the decree of a school board. New presbyter is but old priest write large.

Free schools, to be truly free, must meet two conditions: first, they must be run in a way to prevent the introduction of the hidden curriculum of graded attendance and certified students studying at the feet of certified teachers. And more importantly, they must provide a framework in which all participants, staff and pupils, can free themselves from the hidden foundations of a schooled society. The first condition is frequently stated in the aims of a free school. The second condition is only rarely recognized and is difficult to state as the goal of a free school.

To go beyond the simple reform of the classroom, a free school must avoid incorporating the hidden curriculum of schooling. An ideal free school tries to provide education and at the same time tries to prevent that education from being used to establish or justify a class structure, from becoming a rationale for measuring the pupil against some abstract scale, and from repressing, controlling, and cutting him down to size. But as long as the free school tries to provide 'general education', it cannot move beyond the hidden assumptions of school. Among these assumptions is that which impels us to treat all people as if they were newcomers who had to go through a naturalization process. Only certified consumers of knowledge are admitted to citizenship. Another assumption is that man is born immature and must 'mature' before he can fit into civilized society. Man must be guided away from his natural environment and pass through a social womb in which he hardens sufficiently to fit into everyday life. Free schools can perform this function often better than schools of a less seductive kind.

Free educational establishments share with less free establishments another characteristic. They de-personalize the responsibility for 'education'. They place an institution *in loco parentis*. They perpetuate the idea that 'teaching', if done outside the family, ought to be done by an agency, for which the individual teacher is but an agent. In a schooled society even the family is reduced to an 'agency of acculturation'. Educational agencies which employ teachers to perform the corporate intent of their board are instruments for the de-personalization of intimate relations.

Recovery of Responsibility for Teaching and Learning

A revolution against those forms of privilege and power which are based on claims to professional knowledge must start with a transformation of consciousness about the nature of learning. This means, above all, a shift of reponsibility for teaching and learning. Knowledge can be defined as a commodity only as long as it is viewed as the result of institutional enterprise or as the fulfillment of institutional objectives. Only when a man recovers the sense of personal responsibility for what he learns and teaches can this spell be broken and the alienation of learning from living be overcome.

The recovery of the power to learn or to teach means that the teacher who takes the risk of interfering in somebody else's private affairs also assumes responsibility for the results. Similarly, the student who exposes himself to the influence of a teacher must take responsibility for his own education. For such purposes educational institutions – if they are needed at all – ideally take the form of facility centers where one can get a roof of the right size over his head, access to a piano or a kiln, and to records, books, or slides. Schools, TV stations, theatres, and the like are designed primarily for use by professionals. Deschooling society means above all the denial of professional status for the second-oldest profession, namely teaching. The certification of teachers now constitutes an undue restriction on the right to free speech; the corporate structure and professional pretensions of journalism an undue restriction on the right to free press. Compulsory attendance rules interfere with free assembly. The deschooling of society is nothing less than a cultural mutation by which a people recovers the effective use of its Constitutional freedoms: learning and teaching by men who know they are born free rather than treated to freedom. Most people learn most of the time when they do whatever they enjoy; most people are curious and want to give meaning to whatever they come in contact with; and most people are capable of personal intimate intercourse with others unless they are stupefied by inhuman work or turned off by schooling.

The fact that people in rich countries do not learn much on their own constitutes no proof to the contrary. Rather it is a consequence of life in an environment from which, paradoxically, they cannot learn much, precisely because it is so highly programmed. They are constantly frustrated by the structure of contemporary society in which the facts on which decisions can be made have become more elusive. They live in an environment in which tools that can be used for creative purposes have become luxuries, an environment in which the channels of communication serve a few to talk to many.

A New Technology rather than a New Education
A modern myth would make us believe that the sense of impotence with which most men live today is a consequence of technology that cannot but create huge systems. But it is not technology that makes systems huge, tools immensely powerful, channels of communication one-directional. Quite the contrary: properly controlled, technology could provide each man with the ability to understand his environment better, to shape it powerfully with his own hands, and to permit him full intercommunication to a degree never before possible. Such an alternative use of technology constitutes the central alternative in education.

If a person is to grow up he needs, first of all, access to things, to places, and to processes, to events and to records. He needs to see, to touch, to tinker with, to grasp whatever there is in a meaningful setting. This access is now largely denied. When knowledge became a commodity, it acquired the protections of private property, and thus a principle designed to guard personal intimacy became a rationale for declaring facts

14

off limits for people without proper credentials. In schools teachers keep knowledge to themselves unless it fits into the day's programme. The media inform, but exclude those things they regard as unfit to print. Information is locked into special languages, and specialized teachers live off its retranslation. Patents are protected by corporations, secrets are guarded by bureaucracies, and the power to keep others out of private preserves – be they cockpits, law offices, junkyards, or clinics – is jealously guarded by professions, institutions, and nations. Neither the political nor the professional structure of our societies, East and West, could withstand the elimination of the power to keep entire classes of people from facts that could serve them. The access to facts that I advocate goes far beyond truth in labelling. Access must be built into reality, while all we ask of advertising is a guarantee that it does not mislead. Access to reality constitutes a fundamental alternative in education to a system that only purports to teach *about* it.

Abolishing the right to corporate secrecy – even when professional opinion holds that this secrecy serves the common good – is, as shall presently appear, a much more radical political goal than the traditional demand for public ownership or control of the tools of production. The socialization of tools without the effective socialization of know-how in their use tends to put the knowledge-capitalist into the position formerly held by the financier. The technocrat's only claim to power is the stock he holds in some class of scarce and secret knowledge, and the best means to protect its value is a large and capital-intensive organization that renders access to know-how formidable and forbidding.

It does not take much time for the interested learner to acquire almost any skill that he wants to use. We tend to forget this in a society where professional teachers monopolize entrance into all fields and thereby stamp teaching by uncertified individuals as quackery. There are few mechanical skills used in industry or research that are as demanding, complex, and dangerous as driving cars, a skill that most people acquire quickly from a peer. Not all people are suited for advanced logic, yet those who are make rapid progress if they are challenged to play mathematical games at an early stage. One out of twenty kids in Cuernavaca can beat me at Wiff 'n' Proof after a couple of weeks' training. In four months all but a small percentage of motivated adults at our CIDOC centre learn Spanish well enough to conduct academic business in the new language.

A first step towards opening up access to skills would be to provide various incentives for skilled individuals to share their knowledge. Inevitably, this would run counter to the interests of guilds and professions and unions. Yet multiple apprenticeship is attractive. It provides everybody with an opportunity to learn something about almost anything. There is no reason why a person should not combine the ability to drive a car, repair telephones and toilets, act as a midwife, and function as an architectural draftsman. Special interest groups and their disciplined consumers would, of course, claim that the public needs the protection of a professional guarantee. But this argument is now steadily being challenged by consumer protection associations. We have to take much more seriously the objection that economists raise to the radical socialization of skills: that 'progress' will be impeded if knowledge – patents, skills, and all the rest – is democratized. Their arguments can be faced only if we demonstrate to them the growth rate of futile diseconomies generated by any existing educational system.

Access to people willing to share their skills is no guarantee of learning. Such access is restricted not only by the monopoly of educational programs over learning and of unions over licensing but also by a technology of scarcity. The skills that count today are know-how in the use of tools that were designed to be scarce. These tools produce goods or render services that everybody wants but only a few can enjoy, and which only a limited number of people know how to use. Only a few privileged individuals out of the total number of people who have a given disease ever benefit from the results of sophisticated medical technology, and even fewer doctors develop the skill to use it.

The same results of medical research have, however, also been employed to create a basic tool kit that permits Army and Navy medics, with only a few months of training, to obtain results under battlefield conditions that would have been beyond the expectations of full-fledged doctors during World War II. On an even simpler level any peasant girl could learn how to diag-

16

nose and treat most infections if medical scientists prepared dosages and instructions specifically for a given geographic area.

All these examples illustrate the fact that educational considerations alone suffice to demand a radical reduction of the professional structure that now impedes the mutual relationship between the scientist and the majority of people who want access to science. If this demand were heeded, all men could learn to use yesterday's tools, rendered more effective and durable by modern science, to create tomorrow's world.

Unfortunately, precisely the contrary trend prevails at present. I know a coastal area in South America where most people support themselves by fishing from small boats. The outboard motor is certainly the tool that has changed most dramatically the lives of these coastal fishermen. But in the area I have surveyed, half of all outboard motors that were purchased between 1945 and 1950 are still kept running by constant tinkering, while half the motors purchased in 1965 no longer run because they were not built to be repaired. Technological progress provides the majority of people with gadgets they cannot afford and deprives them of the simpler tools they need.

Metals, plastics, and ferro cement used in building have greatly improved since the 1940s and ought to provide more people with the opportunity to create their own homes. But in the United States, while in 1948 more than 30% of all one-family homes were owner-built, by the end of the 1960s the percentage of those who acted as their own contractors had dropped to less than 20%.

The lowering of the skill level through so-called economic development becomes even more visible in Latin America. Here most people still build their own homes from floor to roof. Often they use mud in the form of adobe and thatchwork of unsurpassed utility in the moist, hot, and windy climate. In other places they make their dwellings out of cardboard, oildrums, and other industrial refuse. Instead of providing people with simple tools and highly standardized, durable, and easily repaired components, all governments have gone in for the mass production of low-cost buildings. It is clear that not one single country can afford to provide satisfactory modern dwelling units for the majority of its people. Yet everywhere this policy makes it progressively more difficult for the majority to acquire the knowledge and skills they need to build better houses for themselves.

Self-chosen 'Poverty'

Educational considerations permit us to formulate a second fundamental characteristic that any post-industrial society must possess: a basic tool kit that by its very nature counteracts technocratic control. For educational reasons we must work toward a society in which scientific knowledge is incorporated in tools and components that can be used meaningfully in units small enough to be within the reach of all. Only such tools can socialize access to skills. Only such tools favour temporary associations among those who want to use them for specific occasions. Only such tools allow specific goals to emerge in the process of their use, as any tinkerer knows. Only the combination of guaranteed access to facts and of limited power in most tools renders it possible to envisage a subsistence economy capable of incorporating the fruits of modern science.

The development of such a scientific subsistence economy is unquestionably to the advantage of the overwhelming majority of the people in poor countries. It is also the only alternative to progressive pollution, exploitation, and opaqueness in rich countries. But as we have seen the dethroning of the GNP cannot be achieved without simultaneously subverting GNE (Gross National Education – usually conceived as manpower capitalization). An egalitarian economy cannot exist in a society in which the right to produce is conferred by schools.

The feasibility of a modern subsistence economy does not depend on new scientific inventions. It depends primarily on the ability of a society to agree on fundamental, self-chosen, anti-bureaucratic and anti-technocratic restraints.

These restraints can take many forms, but they will not work unless they touch the basic dimensions of life. The substance of these voluntary social restraints would be very simple matters that can be fully understood and judged by any prudent man. All such restraints would be chosen to promote stable and equal enjoyment of scientific know-how. The French say that it takes a thousand years to educate a peasant to deal with a cow. It would not take two generations to help all people in Latin

America or Africa to use and repair outboard motors, simple cars, pumps, medicine kits, and ferro cement machines if their design does not change every few years. And since a joyful life is one of constant meaningful intercourse with others in a meaningful environment, equal enjoyment does translate into education.

At present a consensus on austerity is difficult to imagine. The reason usually given for the impotence of the majority is stated in terms of political or economic class. What is not usually understood is that the new class structure of a schooled society is even more powerfully controlled by vested interests. No doubt an imperialist and capitalist organization of society provides the social structure within which a minority can have disproportionate influence over the effective opinion of the majority. But in a technocratic society the power of a minority of knowledge capitalists can prevent the formation of true public opinion through control of scientific know-how and the media of communication. Constitutional guarantees of free speech, free press, and free assembly were meant to ensure government by the people. Modern electronics, photo-offset presses, time-sharing computers, and telephones have in principle provided the hardware that could give an entirely new meaning to these freedoms. Unfortunately these things are used in modern media to increase the power of knowledge bankers to funnel their programme-packages through international chains to more people, instead of being used to increase true networks that provide equal opportunity for the encounter among the members of the majority.

Deschooling the culture and social structure requires the use of technology to make participatory politics possible. Only on the basis of a majority coalition can limits to secrecy and growing power be determined without dictatorship. We need a new environment in which growing up can be classless, or we will get a brave new world in which Big Brother educates us all.

19

IAN LISTER

Getting There from Here

Today many countries in the New World, the Third World, and
the Old World are confronted by a fundamental crisis in Education. From the United States the problems have been chronicled
by people like George Dennison, Paul Goodman, John Holt,
Herbert Kohl, Neil Postman and Charles Weingartner, and
Charles E. Silberman in *Crisis in the Classroom* has written a
protracted lament for the failure of the reform movement during the post-Sputnik era. From Canada we have the radical
analysis and proposals of the Douglas Wright *Report of the
Commission on Post-Secondary Education in Ontario*. In
Africa W. Senteza Kajubi of Uganda has reported that 'the
school system is regarded by many political and educational
leaders as a means of disorientating children from the realities
of life as it is . . .' and he has asked: 'Is the school an obsolete
institution?'; Julius K. Nyerere, President of Tanzania, has
argued that education in his country was such 'as to divorce its
participants from the society it was supposed to be preparing
them for.' From Mexico there are the blueprints for alternatives to Education proposed by Ivan Illich and Everett Reimer.
In many European countries it is commonplace to talk of the
crisis in Education: France has been widely aware of it since
the 'événements' of 1968 and in analysing prospects for Education in the Europe of the future Alain Drouard makes it the
basic point in his argument. It is only in England, with its
lingering belief in conservative reform and the 'flexibility' of the
system, that the schoolmen have gone largely unchallenged.
However, even here the contradictions are becoming more and
more apparent and many of the reformers within the system are
beginning to doubt the ability of the state church of schooling to provide the social salvation it promises: an 'inner emigra-
tion' is forming, and some are looking outside the schools –
towards community action projects in particular – for a way
beyond the present crisis.

Any programme which points to ways beyond that crisis must begin with an analysis of the different aspects of the crisis itself, for this can both explain the failures of the present system and suggest ways ahead. The essence of the crisis is the riddle of mass-education in an urban society. Connected with this is the search for democracy – and for *participatory* democracy. With this, in England, we have a continued concern for the individual. We now recognize cultural diversity in our society – class, racial, and generational cultures – and we believe that a variety of cultures ought not to be suppressed (as in the past) but encouraged. Fundamental to the present crisis of schooling is the growth of a technological, urban, and mobile society. This has seen the decline of such former educators as the extended family, the church, and the community. This has put more strain on social welfare systems – the mobile nuclear family and the rise of the welfare state go hand-in-hand – and, foolishly, schools have taken on more and more tasks which they are unsuited and unable to perform. This in turn has led romantic theorists of traditional 'left' and 'right', such as R. H. Tawney and F. R. Leavis, to look for a way out by idealising communities of the past, and it has led to the ultimate arrogance of the schoolmen who, with the community school movement, have claimed that schools can make the community, and the 'hubris' of some community projects which attempt to create communities through social engineering.

These are only some aspects of the crisis but they go a long way to explaining why the two main contestants in the field of schooling – the élite/academics and the comprehensivists – are both going up the same blind alley. The attempt to democratize an educational system by expanding the élite model is doomed to failure, because élite systems depend not only on those they select but upon the masses they reject and, in terms of social mobility, there is room for just so many cloth caps on the platform of the ruling groups. Comprehensive schools, being institutions, have cultural norms, and they fail to provide for the cultural diversity which exists in our society, or to recognize that different people learn differently and that different individuals have different learning needs. Indeed, as a model of educational provision the comprehensive school is obsolete before it has been achieved. But the élite/academics and the comprehensivists have

21

much more in common than they themselves realize: they are both schoolmen and they share many assumptions: they tend to confuse schooling and education; to believe that learning is the result of teaching, and that learning is a commodity and that knowledge comes in packages processed and purveyed by them. They both believe in 'equality of opportunity' through schooling – which is the central myth of the system – and fail to see that schools cannot create equality of opportunity but only *legitimize* the inequality which exists in society.

The last ten years in England have seen the contradictions of schooling become more and more apparent. The major attempts at reform – with the re-organization of school systems, the introduction of new teaching and learning methods, curriculum development, and the proposed reorganization of teacher training – have, paradoxically, done more to expose the general decay in the mass-service industry of schooling than to remedy it. Like a ramshackle Austro-Hungarian Empire the school system, with the extension of compulsory schooling, has struck out at the very moment of its decline. But the results of the Raising of the School Leaving Age, and the growth of the 'new' sixth-form, have merely exposed the fact that a system which is supposed to cater for everybody has little to offer the majority of its clients which *they themselves* find meaningful. It has also shown that the schoolmen are better at giving new labels to problems ('the Newsom child', 'those below the 60th percentile', 'the socially disadvantaged') than they are at solving them. Thus, while new branches of the schooling industry grow up – the Newsom industry, the deprivation industry, the 'social education' industry – and while that major sector, the curriculum development industry, at last achieves its ultimate aim of in-built obsolescence, we continue to create and colonize third worlds within our own society, and on a national and on a world-wide scale the gap between the rich and the poor grows greater year by year. If aid can mean the economic pacification of poor nations, schooling can all too easily become the social pacification of poor people. It is this which makes the exposure of some of the con-tricks of schooling a moral imperative at the present time. Chief amongst these are that schooling is the same thing as education, and that it can promote equality of opportunity.

22

In searching for a general direction out of the impasse we need to do two things: to draw up the guidelines of an alternative programme and then identify those elements both *inside* and *outside* the present system which could contribute to its realization. Our planning should start from two premisses: that we begin from a theory of man and society and *not* from a theory of knowledge; and that we ask, not the limited question 'How can we keep schools going?' but the general question 'What kind of educational provision ought to exist in our society?' In general, pluralistic provision is the only kind appropriate to a pluralistic society: it is also the only kind which can potentially acknowledge and realize both man's sacred individuality and his social nature. The general lines to get us beyond the present provision, which offers variety but not choice – and which affords alternative provision only to the rich – must include the following three main elements : –

1. An end to compulsion and the promoting of voluntarism. This would also involve the provision of real choice for learners which, in turn, would mean putting the funds, or the credit, for education in their hands, and an expansion of advisory services which would help people to satisfy their need in the more flexible and varied system of the future.

2. Deformalizing instruction and putting more stress on informal and incidental learning – that is learning related to experience. This would mean an end to the schooling system of sequential curricula and graded exercises – a system which fragments reality for the majority of people. It would involve using the resources of the environment – both *things* and *people* – much more than at present.

3. Creating opportunities for life-long learning (permanent education). This would expose the most insidious message of the hidden curriculum of schooling – that education ends when formal schooling ends. It would involve the adequate funding of service-agencies and collaborative enterprises. Only with such provision will readiness for learning and opportunity for learning coincide. Such provision, incidentally, would take pressure off schools which now sometimes foolishly attempt to 'educate for life'. The ultimate aim would be to achieve 'the learning society' which would not only be a society fit for human beings but which would itself be an educational experience.

23

With these essential measures we could begin to dismantle the less effective parts of the present system and achieve two major objectives – the revitalising of non-school education, and getting the responsibility for people's education back into their own hands.

When planning the alternative systems of the future we cannot fail to consider those elements of present provision which might be salvaged, or which might survive because of their appropriateness to the general aim. There is also a very practical point: a famous American bank-robber, when asked why he robbed banks, replied: 'Because that is where the money is.' In the same way the schooling system contains a great, accumulated capital resource in the form of buildings and equipment, and from its human resources it will provide some of the educators of the future. Given the general lines of the programme outlined above one can predict that in the medium term, with the achievement of voluntarism, some schools, like churches, would go out of business and some would survive. In general, those that would survive might include those that offered educational experiences that were not otherwise available in society – such as a hard, academic education, or creative experiences through drama, poetry, painting and sculpture; and those whose provision moved towards, or accorded with, the general spirit of the programme outlined above – i.e. those schools who deschooled themselves by moving away from the traditional stereotype of age-specific groups, compulsory course attendance, teacher-dominated learning systems etc.

In the short run there would be a danger that one kind of school to survive would be the one that sells money and social power in the form of certificates, but as the poor correlation between these certificates and subsequent *academic* performance, and the *negative* correlation between these certificates and subsequent *job* performance became more apparent and more exposed this particular con-trick of schooling would be short-lived. In the society of the future employers themselves will more and more test job applicants according to criteria of job performance *at the time*: one probable consequence of this is that either the kind of courses offered in universities will change, or that there will be fewer applicants for the kind of academic provision now on offer. In the long run the kind of educational service-agencies which will survive will be those which meet the learning needs of the learner, *as felt by the learner* and not as dictated by someone else, and which offer 'worthwhile' activitities which *the learner himself* feels to be worthwhile.

Looking at the Education industry from the inside – both through my involvement in teacher education in England, West Germany and Poland, and by visiting schools all over the country – I cannot be generally optimistic either about the present or the future for schools. However, there are some glimmers of hope. The progressive primary schools of Leicestershire, Oxfordshire, the West Riding and elsewhere may not be as faultless as the American pilgrims who worship at their shrine might suppose, but they do affirm rather than deny human individuality, creativity, and co-operation, and the validity and worth of the pupil's own life and experience.

At the secondary level we are now witnessing some major attempts to relate the school to the 'community', and to regain for compulsory schooling a moral base. Another, more radical approach favoured by Tassinari in Italy and Robinsohn in Berlin is for curricula related to life-situations. At Basingstoke, the new 6th form college offers open access to all young 'people who genuinely desire to continue with their education beyond the age of 16'; it will provide a common core of Main Studies for all students, including field and practical work 'in the broadest sense'. With exploratory learning and a variety of educational enterprises it promises to create for 'a new concept of education for the 16–19 age group.' Others, like Lawrence Stenhouse and John Hipkin, are trying to defend schooling in terms of worthwhile knowledge and worthwhile activities: in particular they stand against the kind of differential curricula which offer hard subjects, and social power, to the minority, and watered-down subjects and social impotence to the majority.

Equally significant, though, are the various projects outside the system, which the system is busy trying to accommodate in some way. These include the Scotland Road Free School in Liverpool which – instead of teaching about labour relations with textbooks or role-playing and simulations – took its pupils to talk to the workers during the sit-in at the Fisher-Bendix works near the city. Its example is being followed by Free Schools in Leeds, Manchester and London. At Liverpool the revived University

Settlement is now running several projects, including 'Check', an advisory service on such matters as welfare rights, landlords, and the law, and an adult literacy scheme based on volunteers. From his base at Bradford Art College Albert Hunt organizes projects of educative drama in which many people can participate. The activities of the educational underground might be revealing to us the outlines of tomorrow's world in that they expose the short-comings of present provision. In many ways these phenomena are more likely to be symptoms of the present crisis that ways beyond it: Free Schools can make people school-dependent as did traditional schools; student community action reflects not only problems in the locality but the desire for students to have a role in society and no longer be the superflous men of our times. Some forms of progressive education – the 'pottery for the workers syndrome', or similar approaches in which therapy is confused with education – are just new ways of selling-out the interests of the mass of the people. In that funds are pre-empted by the traditional institutions many of these projects have to rely on charismatic leaders, sworn to poverty if not to chastity, and it is doubtful whether they will be able both to create a supportive learning environment *and* continuity of provision. In short, we must accept the possibility that schools, like churches, can go on functioning – albeit it with agnostic congregations – long after their vision is dead and their rationale has passed away.

It is this which makes the recent report on Post-Secondary Education in Ontario of such vital importance. Schoolmen, fearing for their pay-packets and their jobs and aware of the shoddy quality of many of the goods they are selling, often dismiss deschooling/alternatives–in–Education programmes as romantic and impractical. Asking what kind of educational provision should exist in their post-industrial society, the Commission also asked: 'Whether we wish to allow the trend toward universal and sequential education to continue, or whether we should provide some viable alternatives?' They came to the major conclusions that 'The Government of Ontario should seek . . . to provide socially useful alternatives . . .' and that these alternatives 'should be funded as realistically and/or generously per individual per annum as are formal types of post-secondary education.' They advocate schemes which combine work and study; which would favour teachers who had experience out-side the cloister of formal educational institutions; where a person could choose to devote a pay-rise to a fund for sub-sequent educational benefits; where the distinction between 'students' and other members of the community would be eradicated, and where the integration of education and society might once again be a reality. The Ontario scheme would involve opening up institutions – such as universities and lib-raries – which already exist, and points to a future in which we would have fewer institutions (which offer value-packages along with their resources), and more service-agencies. Above all, the Ontario Report shows that the creation of alternatives in Edu-cation and of a learning society is a practical proposition.

It is also, of course, a politically dangerous proposition: the genuinely pluralistic society threatens authoritarians of all political parties, and the idea that learners needs a significant say in determining their own learning needs and worthwhile activities threatens those who are now using schooling as a means of political control. The present conceptual crisis, which is part of the crisis in Education, the decay of old institutions, such as schools, political parties, and trade unions, all point to the fact that a cultural revolution is actually happening in our society. In such times teachers, versed in the ideas and trained for the practice of yesteryear are bound to feel insecure. In such situations people can look for authoritarian solutions so that their sense of security – even if it is the security of the prison-house – can be regained. Major changes are bound to take place in our society in the coming years, and at an ever-increasing rate. Thus, it is vital for us to understand the problems, the perils, and the possibilities which now confront us.

One of the greatest dangers facing us is that deschooling could happen, but in ways quite different from those envisaged by Ivan Illich and Everett Reimer. A dissolution of the present school system could lead to a take-over by the international corporations of neo-capitalism. Another is that an alternative programme would be carried into effect in a form of carica-ture. What is most likely is that systems-maintenance organiza-tions and planners will feed elements of deschooling into present systems and, using deschooling labels as a cover, carry on with other programmes. Indeed, if the example of France after 1968 is any indication, we are more likely to see accommodation than confrontation in any 'politique de récupération'.

The future now offers two broad possibilities in schooling and education. On the one hand the diminishing demands of the labour market, with capital-intensive production, might lead to an ever-increasing expansion of the mass service-industry of schooling, creating needs for its own products and validating its own activities. Already Sweden has plans for 'recurrent education' which could end up in this way, and which assumes people will change jobs several times during their lifetime. In this kind of system Education will be run by the Home office (or the Ministry of Internal Security), and the totally schooled society it would produce, with people being subjected to institutional treatment from cradle to grave, would turn the present bad dream of schooling into a lifelong nightmare. The other major possibility is the deschooled society, with a variety of provision, with choice for individuals and groups, in which basic civil rights will be respected. When the world is fit for children and educational agencies are fit for adults we will know that the truly educative society has been achieved.

KEN COATES

Education as a Lifelong Experience

What is the relationship between education and industry? This is a crucial question, but it is quite commonly avoided by educationalists, and particularly by educational reformers. Whenever we do meet it, it is usually to find that those asking it have subtly transformed it in order to assume an answer which is not too discomfiting either to the teaching profession or to industrialists. Of course, the question 'what does industry need from education?' poses quite a different set of problems to those we need to discuss. 'How can education better serve industry?' is the sort of conundrum that arises with every new phase of technological development: more schools, more colleges and universities must be opened to provide more scientists, more administrators, and more technically qualified workpeople, we are told at intervals of about a generation. The priorities in such questions are upside down and back to front. To see things the right way up, and to begin the pursuit of *education,* we must ask 'what sort of factories do our schools need?'

In the abstract, taking formal schooling at its best, there are few teachers who will not, when pushed, lay claim to the fundamental liberal commitment that their role is to stimulate the fullest possible development of their charges. The school, they feel, is properly an incubator of the free personality. That is to say, teachers commonly assume, or to be more accurate, think they assume, that they should treat their students each as an end in himself, and never as a mere means to serve some greater goal: whether that goal be the imagined good of the State, or the anticipated productivity of the Economy, or even, in these agnostic days, the alleged purpose of the Almighty. The old jesuit boast that given care of a child until he reached the age of seven, he would be kept forever in the faith, is seen by the dominant educational consensus of today as almost the very epitome of evil. True, there are some who would explicitly repudiate liberal pretensions, but there are numerous good liberal swearwords to describe the results of such apostasy. 'Indoctrination', 'mani-

29

pulation', 'brain-washing', 'propagandizing' all spring to mind.

To remain on an equally abstract plane, there is not a factory, an office, a mine or a depot in the land in which these basic liberal assumptions can hold sway for a fraction of a moment, not even on Christmas Day when everyone is on holiday. No employer can treat his employees as ends in themselves, whose free personal development is the prime object of his enterprise. Indeed, no employer, however powerful, can easily imagine being so treated himself, even though it is his will, or the will of the élite grouping of which he forms a part, which has determined, often in precise detail, the major life options which are open to, or closed from, his subordinates. Few employers today actually *tell* their workmen that they are paid to work, not to think: but none are able to predicate their activities on any assumption other than that the goals and strategies of the enterprise, insofar as they are determined by anyone at all, must be rigidly monopolized by its directorate. Throughout the majority of modern industry, it is fair to be far more precise than this: individual initiative by an employee is commonly seen as at best an embarrassment, at worst a disruption, while the personal development of employees is considered a matter for their own pursuit, as best they can arrange it, in those parts of their lives which are called 'leisure'. Industry still seeks square pegs for square holes, and round pegs for round holes. Even in the comparatively rare cases where jobs are 'enlarged', or rotated, the modern division of labour remains, for the overwhelming majority of people, an absolute barrier to the development of their productive, or creative, capacities in any field other than the narrow strip to which they have been allotted. Proficiencies which can be learnt in days or weeks frequently become life-expectations. Such horizons can only tend to reduce people, unless they find ways to rebel against them. As Norbert Weiner wrote in *The Human Use of Human Beings*:

'use of a human being in which less is demanded of him than his full stature is a degradation and a waste. It is degradation to a human being to chain him to an oar and use him as a source of power, but it is an almost equal degradation to assign him to a purely repetitive job in a factory, which

30

demands less than a millionth of his brain capacity. It is simpler to organize a factory or a galley which uses human beings for a trivial fraction of their worth than it is to provide a world in which they can grow to their full stature.'

It is no final answer to this problem to turn the galley-slaves, or the wage-slaves, loose for a number of hours a day. The brutalizing of work tends to turn leisure into passivity, or into an aggressively private activity: the alienated antithesis of compulsory labour. Modern industry, modern capitalism, far from constituting a celebration of the freedom of the individual, in fact represents the most systematic and extended denial of the basic conditions of that freedom.

But these are abstract statements, statements moreover of tendency, and they represent only part of the truth. The complex reality is that conditions of unfreedom repeatedly stimulate moods of rejection. Good schools reinforce this rejection, which will only hold out new hopes of fulfilment when subjection no longer remains the rule.

It remains true that the liberal educational goals are, at root, in flagrant contradiction to the basic assumptions which regulate our economic life. The result is that today, far from education – individual development in co-operative activity – reaching out through working life to become a life-long experience, it is still true that industry constantly exerts itself to reach its clammy hands down into the schools, in order to make wage-slavery as life-long, and as inescapable, as it possibly can. Of course, there are gross difficulties in the process. Although it is true that there are still all too many infant schools in which five-year-olds are aligned in ranks in wet playgrounds and whistled into assembly, a ritual which is only meaningful as house-training for the factory and the clocking-in queue, yet it remains quite undeniable that modern pedagogy (which is the more necessary to industry as it desperately roots round to find expanded off-square pegs to fit the new precision-made eccentric holes of modern technology) is persistently rolling back the age at which authoritarian discipline can be introduced. Opening the 1972 Conference of the British National Union of Teachers, the President of the organization claimed that in recent years there had been 'a new spirit in the schools. The primary school today' he said, 'is a place of adventure, experiment, liveliness, joy, and a felicitous co-operation between child, parent and teacher.'

Such progress notwithstanding, and there is still room for a great deal more of it, the school still serves its masters. The more co-operative and participatory that teaching techniques become, the more grossly they will be out of phase with the roles for which their victims are being prepared. The raising of the school leaving age may see a rise in the age of secondary school mutiny: but mutiny remains as likely as ever to nullify even the best pedagogic intentions as the transition from class-room to workshop becomes imminent. In the best imaginable case, if the schools were to succeed in wholly dedicating themselves to the stimulation and liberation of imagination throughout the whole school-life of their pupils, then those pupils would be powerfully tempted to drop out of the society into which they were subsequently evicted. There are reformers, like Paul Goodman, who welcome this prospect. To me it seems an unlikely blessing. Denied access to any satisfactory outlet for productive effort, and denied facilities for creative communication unless they show exceptional talents, such rebels are likely to develop into shallow hedonists, whose lives will be prone to sterile introversion and dependency. If hedonism is a life-style, it is scarcely a *human* life-style: evolution could well have been arrested with the emergence of the common cat, or for all we know, the garden slug, leaving ample possibilities for self-satisfaction at this sad level of expectation. If it were possible for schools to ignore industry during the whole period of compulsory education, and it is not, it would still be ethically impermissible for them to tolerate a factory system which would give their pupils the choice of forgetting the most important things they had learnt, or lapsing into social parasitism. In fact, up to now, this discussion implies, if anything, far too rosy a picture of the state of school autonomy from the industrial power-complex. The whole system of public examinations has no imaginable educational function, but is indispensible to the Labour Exchange. Tests of certain kinds can help both teachers and students: but they help best when the student understands that perhaps their most crucial function is to help the teacher overcome his own inadequacies. There never was a mark awarded that said anything incontrovertible about the ability of a student, because 'ability' is a term which includes a vast area of potential which can never be measured until after it has been realized, and which can (and should) remain open throughout a lifetime: but every mark ever given does say something quite final about the level of actual communication that has taken place between a teacher and his charge. 'Bring out number, weight and measure' said Blake 'in a year of dearth'. The mania for evaluation of students' performance would be a healthy event, if it were a self-critical pedagogic device. As it is, it tends to present a recurrent libel on the capacities of those 'evaluated', which has the effect, all too often, of self-fulfilling prophecy, convincing its victims that *they* suffer from incapacities which are not in truth their own, but their institutions'. Of course, if an employer wants a French-speaking secretary, he has to know that she can in fact speak French before he can employ her. Exams will be with us for a while yet: but we should know for what they were spawned, and refuse them the dignity of an *educational* rationale. Yet, in a negative way, they show us what vast developments are possible, by revealing some fraction of the *needs* which our current school system can never begin to meet. It is precisely when we are confronted by the results of measurements of 'performance' that we become aware of the pervasive influence of social status on the school structure. Poor kids do badly, rich kids do well. As J. W. B. Douglas reports in *The Home and the School:*

'When housing conditions are unsatisfactory, children make relatively low scores in the tests. This is so in each social class, but whereas middle-class children, as they get older, reduce this handicap, the manual working-class children from unsatisfactory homes fall even further behind; for them, overcrowding and other deficiencies at home have a progressive and depressive influence on their test performance.'

Bad housing is important as an indicator of this phenomenon, but its real root is occupational. Unskilled workers are badly paid, which is why they live on poor estates or in slums. Slum housing is certainly a handicap, but it is not an insuperable handicap on its own. Half-blind Sean O'Casey saw more colour in the world from a Dublin tenement than most duchesses can find in a room full of Titians. Abraham Lincoln was reportedly conceived in a log cabin, but his step-mother taught him to read the Bible, *Pilgrim's Progress*, and *Robinson Crusoe*. You have to apply other clamps to the imagination than poor housing if you are to achieve any success in the effort to paralyse it. In British slums, the majority of fathers and mothers have never been introduced to Bunyan or Defoe, or for that matter to any other major writer in our language, so it is hardly surprising if their children read late, and with difficulty. For years it was fashionable to consider this fact as the outcome of genetic determination. The unskilled were not culturally deprived because they were poor and unskilled, but because they were born that way. This was not the view of the classic theorists of industrialism. Adam Smith, who began his greatest work with the celebration of the productive merits of the division of labour, was well aware of its baneful influence on the labourer. His insights on this matter were enlarged in different ways by Owen, Ruskin, and Marx, to say nothing of the whole pleiad of romantic novelists, poets, and publicists. What is perfectly clear is that as factories stabilized themselves as the predominant form of productive unit through society, so the divergence of talents was widened, and transmitted across generations. The industrial division of labour became the solid foundation of an industrial class system. For all its onesidedness, there are few descriptions of this process which are more compelling and more farsighted than that of De Tocqueville, in *Democracy in America:*

'When a workman is unceasingly and exclusively engaged in the fabrication of one thing, he ultimately does his work with singular dexterity; but at the same time he loses the general faculty of applying his mind to the direction of the work. He every day day becomes more adroit and less industrious; so that it may be said of him that in proportion as the workman is improved the man is degraded. . . . When a workman has spent a considerable portion of his existence in this manner, his thoughts are for ever set upon the object of his daily toil; his body has contracted certain fixed habits, which it can never shake off: in a word, he no longer belongs to himself, but to the calling which he has chosen. It is in vain that

34

laws and manners have been at pains to level all barriers around such a man, and to open to him on every side a thousand different paths to fortune: a theory of manufactures more powerful than manners and laws binds him to a craft, and frequently to a spot, which he cannot leave: it assigns him a certain place in society beyond which he cannot go: in the midst of universal movement it has rendered him stationary.

'In proportion as the principle of the division of labour is more extensively applied, the workman becomes more weak, more narrow-minded, and more dependent. The art advances, the artisan recedes. . . .'

This savage prophecy has not been by any means fulfilled in full, for two good reasons. First, for the reason that people *will* resist de-humanization, however high the cost of resistance, and however long the odds against their success. The whole story of trade unionism, and the entire vicarious history of the socialist movement, bear witness to this fact. As a result of it, the basic liberal humanist ideals survive the process which de Tocqueville traced, which is, of course, at one level, itself the result of the operation of the liberal doctrine in economic life. Secondly, the prophecy fails because the story of the development of industrial capitalism is an account of the unleashing of a succession of technological upheavals, during which the division of labour is recurrently recast. On one side this results from time to time in the demand for new skills and higher educational levels: but at the same time, on the other side it repeatedly gives rise to the displacement of old skills and the social rejection of all those people whose inflexibility (whether because they are old, or because they have been inadequately taught in their youth) keeps them below the threshold of profitable employment. So-called technological unemployment is not a new phenomenon, although in its recent forms it has the capacity to create wider unease in the body politic than heretofore. Its true source is not abstract technology, which, being inanimate, is socially neutral, but specific technologies in the service of capital, whose dominance depends upon the control of equipment and processes, and upon the subordination of the interests of people to the imperatives of its balance-sheets.

Adam Smith had adumbrated three component benefits of

the division of labour: it augmented productivity by specialization, increasing the proficiency of workmen by intensifying their dexterity; it saved time by cutting out transfers between operations; and it facilitated the introduction and development of machines. To these three principles, Charles Babbage, in *The Economy of Manufactures,* added a fourth:

'That the master manufacturer, by dividing the work to be executed into different processes, each requiring different degrees of skill and force, can purchase exactly that precise quantity of both of which is necessary for each process.'

With this perception rose the possibility of the whole school of scientific management, as subsequently developed by F. W. Taylor in the United States. The more intensively processes could be controlled, the more dependent roles were created for employees, and the less the industrial currency of the liberal ideal of an integrated human personality. Babbage recorded the process in 1832 without noticing the implication of his words:

'. . . if the whole work were to be executed by one workman, that person must possess sufficient skill to perform the most difficult, and sufficient strength to execute the most laborious, of the operations into which the art is divided.'

Just about fifty years were to elapse before Taylor was to refine this insight to the point where he could insist, without shame, that:

'One of the very first requirements for a man who is fit to handle pig iron as a regular occupation is that he shall be so stupid and so phlegmatic that he more nearly resembles an ox than any other type.'

The logical result of such specialization was clearly expressed in the dire anti-utopia of H. G. Wells' *The Time Machine,* in which exploration of the future revealed that effete aristocrats and feelingless plebians had evolved into two distinct and incompatible species. If the logical result is not to be anticipated in the actual outcome, we owe the fact both to human resilience and to the contradictory implications of advancing techniques. While Taylorism in its classic presciptions gained a considerable following, in spite of protests, in the mass production industries of the Ford school, subsequent work methods have evolved alongside electronic techniques to produce quite different notions of job control. Nevertheless, Taylorism was an innovatory discipline which cast a long shadow before it, and even today, in the discussion of job-enlargement, rotation of tasks, 'participatory' reform, and kindred expedients, the ghost of scientific management can still be heard speaking, in a variety of accents it is true, but with no diminution of its anti-human intent. It is the same ghost which speaks in the debate on educational methods and reform of the schools. 'More means worse', it says. Selection and specialization are its necessary watchwords. Its cardinal principle it transfers from Babbage's factories to the secondary modern schools and the lower streams of the alleged comprehensives which spring up on all sides. 'Spend no more than is necessary on human formation' it whispers. Surplus of training is dysfunctional: overeducated operatives are indisciplined and refractory. In a square hole, square people are optimal, and tendencies to deviate into roundness must be rigidly clamped out.

Yet all the time, industry needs education. A modest explosion has recently taken place in certain forms of continuation courses, in adult classes of a particular kind, in shop steward training, and in technical education, since the passage in Britain of the Industrial Training Act, which levies a toll on firms in order to ensure that if they do not train their own workers, they will be forced to pay to train other people's. A much bigger convulsion is called for, but is unlikely to take place. But all this effort, and most of the proposed effort which will not be undertaken, is conceived within the essential framework of the constricting assumptions we have been discussing. We *could* have a real transformation in education *at* work, but the price would not be simply the universalization of day-release courses, desirable though that may be. A genuine transformation would involve education *in* work, self-education, community education, in the generation of real moves towards collective self-management of industry. Only such a revolution would abolish the stultifying role-patterns which are imposed on workpeople, and only such a revolution would open up the possibility, and the need, for every man to seek the continuous enlargement of his powers and his basic knowledge of the world in which he was working.

Universalist education is incompatible with the rigid division of labour which forms men into porters and philosophers, and aligns them into opposing social classes. Both in work, and in whatever preparation which enlightened people come to agree it may be necessary to make for work, the division of labour as we understand it is more than a net disincentive to free personal development. Within it, 'equality of opportunity' comes to mean the will o' the wisp of an equal start in a fundamentally unequal race: and all the nobility of the watchword is transformed into sleazy apologetics. Free development of each personality to its outer limits means the systematic encouragement and fostering of talents, and this will never begin until factories begin to be schools, and self-governing schools at that. Only then will schools cease to be factories for the engineering of human beings into employees. Perhaps a hundred years ago, this was a utopian message. Today, it is direly practical: the only resource which we possess in virtual abundance is that of human potential, and yet it is that resource which we squander with even greater profligacy than we eat up the earth's finite material resources. Mankind will soon need all the wits and creativity which it is stifling every day in modern industry, and its appendage, modern education, if it is to find the way to live out another century.

COLIN WARD

The Role of the State

How did the state become involved in the first place? Historically, the struggle in Britain to make education free, compulsory and universal, and to keep it out of the exclusive control
of religious organizations, was long and bitter, and the effective opposition to it came, not from libertarian objectors, but
from the upholders of privilege and dogma, as well as from
those (both parents and employers) who had an economic
interest in the labour of children or a vested interest in ignorance. England was in fact a late starter: the notion that primary
education should be free, compulsory and universal is very much
older than the Education Act that was finally passed in 1870.
Martin Luther appealed 'To the Councilmen of all Cities in
Germany that they establish and maintain Christian Schools'
observing that the training children get at home 'attempts to
make us wise through our experience', a task for which life itself
was too short, and which could be accelerated by systematic
instruction by means of books. Compulsory universal education
was founded in Calvinist Geneva in 1536, and Calvin's Scottish
disciple John Knox 'planted a school as well as a kirk in every
parish.' In puritan Massachusetts free compulsory primary
education was introduced in 1647. Friedrich Wilhelm I of
Prussia made primary education compulsory in 1717, and a
series of ordinances of Louis XIV and Louis XV required
regular school attendance in France. The common school, Lewis
Mumford notes, 'contrary to popular belief, is no belated
product of 19th century democracy: it played a necessary part
in the absolutist-mechanical formula... centralized authority
was now belatedly taking up the work that had been neglected
with the wiping out of municipal freedom in the greater part
of Europe.' In other words, having undermined local initiative,
the state was acting in its own interests. Compulsory education
is bound up historically not only with the printing press, the
rise of protestantism and capitalism, but with the growth of the
idea of the nation state itself.

39

All the great rationalist philosophers of the 18th century thought about the problems of popular education, and the two acutest educational thinkers among them ranged themselves on opposite sides on the question of the *organization* of education: Rousseau for the State, William Godwin against it. Rousseau, whose *Emile* postulates a completely individual education (human society is ignored, the tutor's entire life is devoted to poor Emile), did nevertheless, in his *Discourse on Political Economy* (1758) argue for public education 'under regulations prescribed by the government . . . if children are brought up in common in the bosom of equality; if they are imbued with the laws of the State and the precepts of the General Will . . . we cannot doubt that they will cherish one another mutually as brothers . . . to become in time defenders and fathers of the country of which they will have been for so long the children.'

Godwin, in his *Enquiry Concerning Political Justice* (1793) criticises the whole idea of a *national* education. He summarises the arguments in favour, which are those used by Rousseau, adding the question, 'If the education of our youth be entirely confined to the prudence of their parents, or the accidental benevolence of private individuals, will it not be a necessary consequence that some will be educated to virtue, others to vice, and others again entirely neglected?' Godwin's answer is worth quoting at length because his lone voice from the end of the 18th century speaks to us in the accents of the deschoolers of our own day:

> The injuries that result from a system of national education are, in the first place, that all public establishments include in them the idea of permanence . . . public education has always expended its energies in the support of prejudice; it teaches its pupils not the fortitude that shall bring every proposition to the test of examination, but the art of vindicating such tenets as may chance to be previously established. . . . Even in the petty institution of Sunday schools, the chief lessons that are taught are a superstitious veneration for the Church of England, and to bow to every man in a handsome coat. . . .
>
> Secondly, the idea of national education is founded in an inattention to the nature of mind. Whatever each man does

40

for himself is done well; whatever his neighbours or his country undertake to do for him is done ill. . . . He that learns because he desires to learn will listen to the instructions he receives and apprehend their meaning. He that teaches because he desires to teach will discharge his occupation with enthusiasm and energy. But the moment political institution undertakes to assign to every man his place, the functions of all will be discharged with supineness and indifference. . . .

Thirdly, the project of a national education ought uniformly to be discouraged on account of its obvious alliance with national government. . . . Government will not fail to employ it to strengthen its hand and perpetuate its institutions. . . . Their view as instigator of a system of education will not fail to be analogous to their views in their political capacity. . . .

Contemporary critics of the alliance between national government and national education would agree, and would declare that the idea that there is a *positive* role for the state in a system of education without schools betrays a complete misunderstanding of what the argument is about: that it is the *nature* of public authorities to run coercive and hierarchical institutions, whose ultimate function is to perpetuate social inequality and to brainwash the young into acceptance of their particular slot in the organized system. A hundred years ago the anarchist Michael Bakunin characterized 'the people' in relation to the state as 'the eternal minor, the pupil confessedly forever incompetent to pass his examination, rise to the knowledge of his teachers, and dispense with their discipline.'

Today we would add a further criticism of the role of the state as educator throughout the world : the affront to the idea of social justice. An immense effort by well-intentioned reformers has gone into the attempt to modify the system to provide equality of opportunity, but this has simply resulted in a theoretical and illusory equal start in a competition to become more and more unequal. The greater the amount of money that is poured into the education systems of the world, the less it benefits the people at the bottom of the educational, occupational and social hierarchy. The universal education system turns out to be yet another way in which the poor subsidise the rich.

Everett Reimer, for instance, remarking that schools are an almost perfectly regressive form of taxation, notes that the children of the poorest one-tenth of the population of the United States cost the public in schooling $2,500 each over a lifetime, while the children of the richest one-tenth cost about $35,000. 'Assuming that one-third of this is private expenditure, the richest one-tenth still get ten times as much of public funds for education as the poorest one-tenth.' In his suppressed Unesco pamphlet of 1970, Michael Huberman reached the same conclusion for the majority of countries in the world. In Britain, ignoring completely the university aspect, we spend twice as much on the secondary school life of a grammar-school sixth-former as on a secondary modern school leaver, while if we do include university expenditure it is calculated in *Labour and Inequality* (London: Fabian Society 1972) that we spend as much on an undergraduate in one year as a normal schoolchild throughout his life. 'While the highest social group benefit *seventeen* times as much as the lowest group from the expenditure on universities, they only contribute five times as much revenue.' We may thus conclude that one significant role of the state in the national education systems of the world is to perpetuate social and economic injustice.

But is the national education system in Britain a state system? The fact is that not a single school in Great Britain is owned or run by the state. They are owned and maintained (with the exception of independent and 'direct grant' schools) by local education authorities. The local authorities draw their income from the rates (a local tax on the occupation of property) but as these have to be boosted to meet present day levels of expenditure by grants from the central government, the state has an effective, but hidden, check on the activities of local authorities. In spite of this theoretical decentralization, our schools are fundamentally alike, not only in terms of Ivan Illich's definition of school as the 'age-specific, teacher-related process requiring full-time attendance at an obligatory curriculum' but in a thousand details of institutional management and goals. However the British decentralized system *is* significant for the strategist of experiment in education without schools because if he is to get official help or sponsorship or even toleration for a radical experiment, it is the local education authority that he has to contend with, and local pressure is a lot easier and can gain a great deal more local interest and support, than attempts to chip away at the monolithic Department of Education and Science.

The key point in discussing alternative education in relation to the official system in Britain, as in most countries, is that options have been pre-empted by the fact that every householder and every taxpayer is compelled to finance the system as it exists. Not only does this *fait accompli* inhibit the development of alternatives, but it also means that these alternatives are dependent on the marginal income of potential users, over and above the compulsory levy to maintain the organized system. Having more marginal income at their disposal, the rich, unlike the poor, are able to make this choice and send their children to independent schools. (John Vaizey calculated that one third of the cost of education in the private sector was recouped through tax avoidance.) Some of the not-so-rich do so as well, out of the conviction that they are doing their best for their children, or because they have mastered the know-how on ways in which their children can earn scholarship places. But of course most 'independent' schools – the exception being the tiny handful of 'progressives' – are identical in all significant features with those in the official system, the important difference being that of class size.

Radical critics of the official system can adopt one of three attitudes. The first is to press for syphoning off into alternative systems a share of educational expenditure and facilities. The second is to attempt to modify the system either by subversion from within or pressure from without. The third is to go it alone, ignoring the official system but continuing, presumably, to finance it through rates and taxes. In practice we are likely to embrace all three attitudes at the same time. For example, when John Ord and his friends set up the Scotland Road Free School in Liverpool, they quickly found it necessary to seek assistance from the local education authority. This was thought irresistibly funny by the educational journalists, but it was perfectly logical. If the parents had opted for a Catholic education it would have been financed by the local authority. If they had opted for a Direct Grant grammar school (and if their children had succeeded in gaining admission) their education would have been financed by the central government. Why should not the Free School, or any deschooling experiment, qualify for the money which the Liverpool Corporation would otherwise have been spending on its students? (All it asked for in fact was accommodation, school meals and furniture, and all it got was a loan of secondhand tables and chairs.) One member of the Education Committee declared that 'If we are being asked to support the school we are being asked to weaken the fabric of what we ourselves are supposed to be supporting.... We might finish up with the fact that no children will want to go to our schools.'

An illuminating remark. It underlines the fact that for the ordinary parent the 'freedom of choice' which exists in theory, is in fact spurious, and it underlines the monopolistic character of the official system. You can see why Illich calls for the 'dis-establishment' of education on the analogy of the dis-establishment of religion. He and people very far from his point of view are attracted by an idea which has been canvassed since the nineteen-fifties by a number of educational economists of both left and right: the notion of education vouchers. Put at its simplest, this suggests that each citizen at birth receives an actual or notional book of vouchers or coupons which entitles him to so many units of education which can be bought at any time in his life. The vouchers represent his share of the nation's educational budget. When he is a child his parents might spend some vouchers at the local primary school, or at a private school or non-school, or might not spend them at all and let Johnny learn to read at home or from his peers. When he is fourteen he might spend his vouchers at the local comprehensive or Eton or the Scotland Road Free School, or he might get a job as an errand boy or shelf-filler at the supermarket, or apprentice himself, surrendering some coupons, to the local electrical engineer. At eighteen he might go to a university or to the technical college, or on an archeological dig, or he might save his coupons until he is thirty, forty, or fifty, or whenever he felt motivated to buy a new educational experience. If he spent all his coupons he could pay cash.

This is a widely attractive idea. It appeals to those who would like to see a genuine freedom of choice with competition on equal terms between radically different kinds of learning, and who want to see the education market more responsive to the expressed needs of students. It appeals to those who find it ludicrous that for most people 'education' is confined to the school system and to the first decade-and-a-half of life, and who think that access to 'higher' education should not be confined to an élite in late adolescence (which may very well be quite the wrong stage of life for it), but should be available throughout life at the time or times when people feel a need for it, for either occupational or personal reasons. It appeals to those who want to preserve the interests of the rich who see themselves as hard done by because while they buy educational privilege for their own children in the private sector, they have to pay the share that the County Treasurer and the Chancellor decide to take from them for the education of everyone else. Yet it appeals also to those who cherish the interests of the poor, because they *know* that in fact the existing system is yet another way in which the poor subsidize the rich.

A voucher system would not in itself end élitism – the restriction of entry into occupations through educational qualification: it would need a revolution to do that. But it would facilitate a whole range of alternative experiments which today are strangled at birth for lack of their share of educational finance. As there is no sign of any government actually adopting anything like a voucher system, we have to look for ways in which the decentralized structure of the existing system can be exploited to provide genuine alternatives. The best existing example is that of the *Friskoler* or free schools in Denmark, which exploit the legislation originally made to provide for municipal support for religious education, to run small parent-controlled schools with the aid of subsidies from the local authorities. Similar premises exist in Britain in the form of the primary and secondary schools instituted by various religious bodies and known as 'voluntary' schools. It would be an interesting exercise in legal gamesmanship to set up in some area where schools were overcrowded a secular 'voluntary' school and to fight through the tangle of educational legislation to get it adopted as a 'controlled, aided, or special agreement school.'

In the early nineteen-sixties, Paul Goodman listed half a dozen experiments which a school board or local education authority could adopt if it were bold enough. They were (in slightly condensed form):

1. Have 'no school at all' for some classes (no academic harm since there is good evidence that normal children will make up the first seven years of school work with four to seven months of good teaching).
2. Dispense with the school building for a few classes; provide teachers and use the city itself as a school.
3. Both outside and inside the school building, use appropriate *unlicensed* adults of the community – the druggist, the storekeeper, the mechanic – as the proper educators of the young into the grown-up world.
4. Make class attendance not compulsory, in the manner of A. S. Neill's Summerhill.
5. Decentralize an urban school into small units of 20–50, in available store-fronts or clubhouses.
6. Use a *pro rata* part of the school money to send children to economically marginal farms for a couple of months a year.

The first of these is a non-starter. It might be popular with the kids, but parents would obviously feel that they were being sold short. The last would probably be interpreted as a cheap labour racket. But several of the others have been adopted successfully by American school boards and have application in Britain: the storefront school is an obvious candidate for adoption.

The idea of the school without walls, for example, has been put into practice for over three years by the Parkway Education Program in the city of Philadelphia with the full support of the education authority. Students are not hand-picked, but are chosen by lottery amongst applicants from the eight geographically-determined school board districts of the city, and are in grades 9–12 (i.e. ages 14–18) regardless of academic or behavioural background. There is no school building. Each of the eight units (which operate independently) has a headquarters with office space for staff and lockers for students. All teaching takes place within the community: the search for facilities is considered to be part of the process of education. 'The city offers an incredible variety of learning labs: arts students study at the Art Museum, biology students meet at the zoo; business and vocational courses meet at on-the-job sites such as journalism at a newspaper, or mechanics at a garage. . . .' The Parkway Program claims that 'although schools are supposed to prepare for a life in the community, most schools so isolate students from the community that a functional understanding of how it works is impossible. . . . Since society suffers as much as the students from the failures of the educational system, it did not seem unreasonable to ask the community to assume some responsibility for the education of its children.' Any British local education authority could set up a Parkway project tomorrow if it wished.

But the likeliest lever for change, in propelling local education authorities into the support or inception of deschooling experiments, will not be example or criticism from outside, but pressure from below. The mass of recalcitrant and rebellious pupils imprisoned in the system for another year by the raising of the minimum leaving age, will be the most powerful argument for change. There has always been a proportion of pupils who attend unwillingly, who resent the authority of the school and its arbitrary regulations, and who put a low value on the processes of education because their own experience tells them that it is an obstacle race in which they are so often the losers that they would be mugs to enter the competition. They learnt *this* lesson at school, which they couldn't wait to enter at five and can't wait to get out of at fifteen. What will happen when this army of also-rans, no longer cowed by threats, no longer amenable to cajolery, no longer to be bludgeoned by physical violence into sullen acquiescence, grows large enough to prevent the traditional school from functioning with even the semblance of efficiency? Sir Alec Clegg has held out this prospect before us for years as a warning that we should change our social and educational priorities. The crisis of authority in education will make de-schoolers of us all, teachers and classes alike, united in the demand to be somewhere else.

All those little local initiatives for truancy centres, community workshops and alternatives to school, will then be seized upon by the authorities and supported by them, *not* because they will have been converted to a different educational philosophy, but as an expedient for keeping the kids off the streets and out of the schools, which themselves will be delighted to be rid of those elements which prevent them from getting on with the task of grooming the more docile students for their place in the certificated meritocracy. I fear that the same is true of the idea of the creative role for the official education system in the development of out-of-school education for a leisured society: its practical application would simply be as occupational therapy for the permanently unemployed.

It is foolish to attempt to persuade the various Ministries of Education or of Public Instruction throughout the world to dissolve the system, a system that reflects and protects the values of the state. It is like expecting the withering away of the state to come by Act of Parliament. Nor should we fall into the trap, having identified the state as a restrictive institution for the protection of privilege, of demanding that legislation be enacted to forbid educational discrimination. What we should be demanding is the right of alternative educational procedures to compete on equal terms. When the Emperor asked the philosopher what he should do, the philospher replied, 'Just move over a little. You're standing in my light.'

MICHAEL ARMSTRONG

The Role of the Teacher

In September 1862, in the ninth number of his educational magazine Yasnaya Polyana, Tolstoy published an article with this title: 'Should we teach the peasant children to write or should they teach us?' In the same month he was married; in less than a year the magazine was wound up and the school he had established for peasant children on his estate was more or less abandoned. As one of his former pupils wrote half a century later, 'At that period Lev Nikolayevitch was writing some big book or other.' The book was *War and Peace*.

Tolstoy's article is one of the most astonishing essays ever written about education. In it he describes in passionate detail 'how I inadvertently hit upon the right method' of teaching children to write. He had suggested that the children might write a story about the proverb 'He feeds you with a spoon and pokes you in the eye with the handle'. One of them said 'Write it yourself'. As he wrote the children began to come up, look over his shoulder, and criticise his writing. Before long he was no longer writing his own story, but acting as the scribe for the story they told him to write. Two boys in particular took over the work and in the end it became, simply, their story. Tolstoy was overwhelmed: 'The next day I could still not believe what I had experienced the day before. It seemed to me so strange that a semi-literate peasant boy should suddenly evince such a conscious artistic power as Goethe, on his sublime summit of development, could not attain. It seemed so strange and insulting that I, the author of *Childhood,* which had earned a certain success and recognition for artistic talent from the educated Russian public, that I, in a matter of art, not only could not instruct or help the eleven-year-old Syomka and Fyedka, but only just – and then only in a happy moment of inspiration – was I able to follow and understand them.'

I hope that Tolstoy's confession, or proclamation, will not seem too eccentric an introduction to an essay on the role of the teacher. For my argument will rest on the assumption that every teacher who wishes to respect the autonomy of his students is forced to take Tolstoy's question, and his confession, seriously. To contemplate, rigorously and without sentimentality, the proposition that in the pursuit of knowledge and truth the roles of teacher and pupil are often reversible, requires a degree of radicalism that even the most committed amongst them find hard to practise.

It is not simply a matter of abandoning the teacher's traditional authoritarianism, although even so obvious a preliminary is harder to achieve than it seems. Authoritarianism is grounded in more than a set of institutional rules, a body of sanctions, or an ultimate reliance on legal, moral, or physical compulsion. It is implicit within the teacher's language and style, as Douglas Barnes elegantly demonstrates in *Language, the Learner and the School*. Few, if any, teachers are aware of the extent of the authoritarianism hidden within the way we talk to our pupils, question, or praise them. Nor do we yet fully appreciate how far the same authoritarianism is implicit within the style, and perhaps the structure of the subjects, disciplines, and bodies of knowledge which we teach. Indeed it seems likely that authoritarianism would easily survive the abolition of schools as institutions, so central a part does it play in our understanding of teaching.

Take, for example, the way in which we as teachers make use of the child's own experience. I teach in a school – Countesthorpe Community College, in Leicestershire—which believes itself, correctly I think, to be progressive. We believe that our students should be autonomous, responsible for directing their own course of learning with our help. In trying to create conditions in which autonomy might thrive we place our emphasis on working outwards from the individual child's immediate experience and concern. Yet often, on reflection, our interest in the child's individual experience is more apparent than real. At any rate we often seem disinterested in the child's experience for its own sake: all our attention is directed towards what, as teachers, *we* can make out of a child's experience. Our aim is to use his experience largely as a starting point in the process of leading him forward from where *he* is at present to where *we* are at present. There is only one direction. Understanding, truth, authority are somehow still seen as inevitably on the teacher's side.

The same unacknowledged authoritarianism lurks behind many of our attempts at curriculum planning. A theme is chosen, strategies worked out to relate it to the pupils' experience and interests, materials prepared, resources mobilized. The process is intensely exciting, above all, I think, because it incites us to pursue ourselves the course of study we are preparing to advocate to our pupils. Ironically, by the time the programme is ready to be presented to the pupils for whom it is intended, our own enthusiasm as teachers is often half-spent, or else has become so self-absorbing that we cannot appreciate that it will not be shared by everyone else. We have become our own curriculum's ideal pupils: our resources are beautifully designed to satisfy not our pupils' intellectual demands, but our own.

The flaw is simple and fatal. Even the best curricula, nationally and within the individual school, however free, are typically designed by teachers for pupils, not by teachers and pupils for each other. But planning a curriculum, at its best, is identical to pursuing a course of study, and the final curriculum should be no more than the finished pursuit. When we, as teachers, take charge of the planning we are effectively, if not intentionally, demanding that our pupils shall pursue *our* course of studies rather than their own.

The solution is as simple as the problem. If pupils are to be free to direct their own course of study with the help of their teachers, they have to be equally free to prepare their own curricula. *Planning* a curriculum becomes as collaborative an enterprise between teacher and pupil as *following* a curriculum. Strictly, perhaps, the two aspects of curriculum are inseparable, which is not to say that studying a subject entails no preparation. The curriculum becomes no more, and equally no less, than the history of a collaborative experience of learning.

The inconsistencies in at any rate my own experience of progressive education spring from our reluctance to take seriously enough the question posed by Tolstoy – who should teach whom? But before returning to it, in order to explore the question's implications for the teacher's role, I want to note three interpretations of that role which seem to be implicit in many discussions of progressive theory and practice. Each interpreta-

51

tion contains a hidden element of the authoritarianism I have already discussed.

The first is that which sees the teacher's role as fundamentally one of providing resources, and managing and monitoring the student's subsequent learning. The teachers provide as richly suggestive an environment for learning as they can, and set their pupils free to explore it as they wish. The trouble is that this interpretation leaves too much both to the teacher and to his pupils. The teacher exclusively prepares the learning environment which, as I have already suggested, is more likely to reveal his own preoccupations than those of his pupils. By leaving his pupils alone to explore as they wish what *he* has created, he compounds the error by making it impossible for collaboration to take place either in the initial preparation or the subsequent learning. A similar mistake is made by those who believe that teachers might be replaced by programmes, computers, television series, or learning packages – a world of 'knowledge' processed afar from the student without his participation.

The second interpretation preserves the traditional role of the teacher, but seeks to rid it of authoritarianism by letting the pupil decide whether or not to attend lessons and courses. It is a familiar interpretation to anyone who has had experience of the now traditional 'progressive' public school. The pattern of the individual lesson, as of the syllabus as a whole, remains much the same as in a more authoritarian public school, but the pupil no longer is forced to attend. Freedom to stay away from classes, like freedom to stay away from school, is not necessarily insignificant, but neither is it in itself sufficiently important. In particular, the teacher who preserves a traditional style and content while abandoning a traditional compulsion is likely to conceal, behind his formal permissiveness, an authoritarian structure of knowledge and thought. His interest in his students' freedom is more apparent than real.

There is a third interpretation of the teacher's role which appears to deny all authority whatever to the teacher. It is far more commonly found in progressive theory than practice, and especially in interpretations of the theory by its critics. This is the view that the teacher must accept more or less every decision his students make, without serious question – that he must put himself totally at their service. And, indeed, when first we try to rid ourselves of an authoritarian past it is hard not to assume that every decision of our pupils is acceptable, if only because we know how deep-seated is our instinct to force them into a 'willing' acceptance of our own decisions. Nonetheless the slack permissiveness of this attitude is, in its turn, as authoritarian as the purely formal permissiveness of the second interpretation. For our refusal as teachers to oppose any decision our pupils make is usually a symptom of our failure to take their experience seriously. To treat another person's experience seriously – as seriously as we treat our own – entails a readiness to challenge it. Teachers who have given up challenging their pupils at any point must also have given up the attempt to learn and teach collaboratively. By refusing to challenge his pupils the teacher is, perhaps, consciously or not, seeking to preserve his own experience from being challenged.

Who, then, should teach whom? There are moments in Tolstoy's essay when he too seems to be implying that the pupil is always right, the teacher invariably at fault. And the whole burden of his essay is to demonstrate that his pupils possessed an artistic power and truth which could rival and surpass those very qualities for which he was himself most admired. Most readers find it impossible to believe that Tolstory really meant that his pupils wrote better than he did. To treat the experience and thought our pupils express as equal or superior to our own at first requires a suspension of our disbelief. But it is clear from a reading of Tolstoy's essay that his question – who should teach whom – is not meant to be answered one way or the other. Neither teacher nor pupil has primacy over the other: their roles are interchangeable. Education becomes a collaborative exercise in learning or, perhaps more fundamentally, a collaborative pursuit of knowledge and truth, in which each side recognizes the special position of the other.

In *Letter to a Teacher* the pupils of the School of Barbiana describe the mutual advantages and disadvantages of a boy educated in an elementary school and one educated at college. This description may serve as a last image of the divisions which collaborative learning sets out to heal.

'Unlucky Gianni who can't express himself. Lucky Gianni

because he belongs to the whole world: brother to the whole of Africa, Asia, and Latin America. Expert in the needs of most of humanity.

'Lucky Pierino, because he can speak. Unlucky, because he speaks to much. He, who has nothing important to say. He, who repeats only things read in books written by others just like him. He, who is locked up in a refined little circle – cut off from history and geography.'

So teacher and pupil should teach each other and learn from each other, making use of each other's strengths and weaknesses in a joint exploration. What, then, is the teacher's particular role in this collaboration and how can he best perform it?

Whatever he does he must attempt to preserve the autonomy of his students – their right, and, equally, their ability to exercise that right, to determine their own education in collaboration with the teacher. I have already suggested the degree of difficulty in ridding ourselves of our authoritarian past as teachers. It is hardly surprising that at first we tend to follow wherever our pupils lead, though we may be unclear about the direction. My own experience is that this abdication of the teacher's role is quickly perceived, both by teachers and pupils, as an attempt to deny the teacher's responsibility as collaborator. But once we ask ourselves precisely what that responsibility is, we immediately run into difficulty.

Self-directed learning presents the teacher with a paradox. For a pupil to direct his own learning successfully he needs access to an abundance of activities, experiences, and subject matters, presented to him with energy and enthusiasm, between which he can choose and select. And that suggests access to an abundance of specialist teachers, experts in particular subject matters, zestfully committed to whatever it is they are teaching. The strength of Tolstey's passion for literature made him a far better teacher of writing than mathematics, and far more responsive to his pupils' literary strengths. Yet for a pupil to direct his own learning successfully he also needs close and systematic help and guidance from teachers who know him well – his interests, attitudes, values, abilities, quirks – and whom he knows equally well. And that suggests teachers who know him and work with him not simply as a student of literature or mathematics but in a much more open context – generalists rather than specialists. Thus Tolstoy's profound understanding of his pupils' love of art arose out of a context in which he did, after all, also teach them mathematics, and science, and physical education, and in which he spent long hours simply talking with them or listening to them or working alongside them. How then can the widest range of opportunities be reconciled with the closest personal relationship between pupil and teacher?

Not, I believe, by separating and isolating the two roles of pastoral guidance and specialist teaching. In his book *Deschooling Society* Ivan Illich draws a distinction between 'pedagogues' and 'educational leaders' or 'masters'. The pedagogue's role is to help pupils to determine their educational goals, to give them insight into the difficulties they encounter, to help them choose between different ways of achieving their ends. The 'master's' role is to 'act as primus inter pares in undertaking difficult intellectual exploratory journeys'. To separate these two roles and allocate them to different people seems to me to be a profound mistake. It is an extension, in the context of a deschooled society, of what many comprehensive schools already try to do when they distinguish between a tutorial system of *pastoral* guidance, and an *academic* system of subject teaching. The division has proved unsatisfactory even within the relatively closed system of the traditional school, and is still less suited to the open system of free schools or to a deschooled society. For although educational guidance and intellectual leadership are distinguishable activities, they are inseparable aspects of teaching.

Guidance is paramount. Without the systematic help of tutors or pedagogues only a few students are likely to direct their own learning successfully. Wherever education assumes the autonomy of the student, the tutorial role becomes the teacher's central part in the education of his students. But the tutorial role cannot be seen as that of some sort of educational consultant. In order to be equipped to offer sustained and systematic guidance to his pupils a tutor needs to know them, as students and as people, and in order to know them he needs to study with them as well as talk to them or observe them. On the one hand he needs to study with them across the widest possible range of intellectual pursuits, for how else can he hope to spot the full range of opportunities from which the individual student might profit. On the other hand he needs to undertake with them precisely those 'difficult intellectual exploratory journeys' in which his own passion and strength is most committed and most at risk. It is just such journeys which draw the teacher and the pupil most closely together. By this means, above all, a tutor comes to know his pupils best and hence to help them best.

The closest contemporary society comes to presenting us with a model of teaching which reconciles educational guidance with intellectual leadership is in the primary school. At her best the primary school teacher working in a more or less progressive English primary school is perhaps the only contemporary polymath, even if to herself she seems more like a jack of all trades. She is something of an expert in the psychology of learning and the nature of childhood, passionately committed to intellectual exploration within the most widely ranging areas of experience, rarely afraid to tackle, at the invitation of her pupils, new disciplines, and often the master of some particular part of the experience which she teaches – art or nature or language. Doubtless to put it so baldly is to idealize, but it is an idealization which is drawn from life. Primary school teachers, and perhaps also some secondary school teachers of English, are the only figures, at any rate within our present educational system, who are already capable of combining within themselves the roles of educational guidance and intellectual leadership. As far as primary school teachers are concerned I would guess that this is partly a product of their experience of working in schools where a relative freedom for pupils is already almost traditional (though it should be added that the genuinely progressive primary school is still comparatively rare in Britain), but partly also a reflection of the training they have received at Colleges of Education. However glaring their weaknesses, such Colleges at their best still offer an education which is far superior to that of the university, or even, I believe, the polytechnic.

However, even on an idealized level, primary school teachers find it hard to do all things equally well. When you wander into a junior school classroom and spend some time there, working with the teacher and the children and watching them, you commonly find that certain areas of experience are far more powerfully represented within that classroom than others. The room is stuffed with science and art and mathematics maybe, but empty of poetry, or full of literature but lacking mathematics or music. Sometimes, then, if you wander into someone else's classroom in the same school, you may observe that what was missing in the one room is richly present in the other. If the obvious solution seems to be to combine the two classes, the experience of primary schools suggests that in practice it is not quite as simple. Two teachers with 70 pupils do not necessarily work as well as each of them with 35. Even so, at least each class would gain from a much more open access to each other, from some sharing of strength. And this suggests in turn a more general solution to the problem of combining educational guidance with intellectual leadership.

For, if it is impossible for one teacher on his own to reconcile fully within his own person these two teaching roles, it is much easier, I believe, to envisage a small group of teachers doing so if they and their students chose to work closely together. Indeed I cannot envisage the reconciliation of roles except in such a context. I imagine a small group of teachers, three or four or five, working with a group of some hundred pupils, more or less. (Precise figures are irrelevant despite the furious comitment so often attached to them.) The purpose of their working together is to undertake Illich's 'difficult intellectual exploratory journeys'. The role of the teachers in this joint enterprise is to help their pupils to discover which journeys they should undertake and to offer their accumulated experience, knowledge and skill, whether as leaders, guides, or followers, on whatever journeys the students select. They are part pedagogue, part master, part fellow pupil, part interested spectator: none of these roles is wholly separable from the others and none can be simply hived off to outsiders. The new teachers, like the new structures of thought towards which in the long run a new education would lead, must be protean figures.

In a society in which the educational system respected the student's autonomy, such small co-operative cells would be at the centre of the educational process, whether that process took place in institutions like schools or outside them. In a sense, therefore, it seems as if schools must be abolished in order to resurrect them. In their contemporary form, schools as institutions are probably incapable of respecting the individual

57

student's autonomy. Yet my argument is that such autonomy cannot be fully respected except through the medium of something like a school, if only in miniature – a small group of teachers and pupils voluntarily working together on a collaborative exercise in learning.

No one teaching group, however, could hope or wish to be self-sufficient. There would necessarily be a wide range of intellectual pursuits in which none of the teachers was able to offer a mastery accumulated over a period of time, however eager they might be to join the pursuit themselves with their students. Besides, if the intellectual journeys the group undertook were not nourished by outside experience, as indeed is the case in modern schools, many of them would be unlikely to land up anywhere. Each group therefore would need access to outside specialists, masters of their art or science or particular skill, who could offer pupils, and their teachers, both their advice and their participation. Such specialists, part consultants and part directors, would most often be people who were not, in their working lives, primarily concerned with education. They would include academics, artists, sportsmen, experts in particular jobs or professions, or parents with particular skills and interests. Just as the contemporary university teacher, more often in theory than practice, divides his time between teaching and research, so might many other workers, in varying degrees. Sometimes the specialist would bring the students out of their group to work with him, sometimes he would go into the group to work. In either case it would be important for the group's teachers, as well as their pupils, to be able to work with the specialist, partly in order to help both pupils and specialists to understand each other better and partly to increase the range and depth of their own intellectual mastery. For the teacher, collaboration with the specialist would be one more aspect of his own continuing education.

No teaching group would be self-contained either. While each would need some sort of base – a shop, house, huts or something more definably like a school – much of the group's work would take place outside it, in museums, libraries, factories, streets, laboratories, offices, shops, countryside. As much as anything it is the isolation of the school from its environment which has ensured its rejection by its pupils, though in the changed

58

circumstances of a freer and more open context, isolation would be seen to have its advantages too.

Joining a group would be voluntary, in a free system of education, and it would not be the only available educational option. Some students who joined a particular group would eventually, before they came to the end of whatever full time education they wanted, choose to continue their education outside the group context, attaching themselves, as apprentices, to particular specialists, or working on their own without further guidance from teachers. A few might, from a relatively early age, prefer to direct their own education by themselves, making use of teachers simply for advice on resources, or as experts in partticular disciplines. In other words, for a few students, the separation of the roles of guidance and educational leadership might be exactly what they wanted. I suspect however that such examples would be relatively rare. For most students the bulk of whatever formal education they received, from early childhood to adolescence, would probably take place within the overall environment of the teaching group or cell.

I am well aware of the host of problems still left on one side in my argument, let alone the central issue of how to get from where we are now to where I have tried to suggest we ought to be. I have said nothing, for example, about how to find and train teachers for their central role. Many of them might come into teaching from other jobs and stay in it for only relatively short periods, five or six years, at any one time. No present form of certification would be more than marginally relevant to their selection. As for their training much, if not most, of it would take place on the job, newcomers working with more experienced teachers and with students of the processes of learning who were working on their researches within the teaching groups. Nor have I said anything about how to provide the groups with the resources they will require, although it is certain that no group could afford to be self sufficient in this regard. Finally I have not indicated how children and their parents might choose which group to join and have access to all the information they would require in order to make a rational choice. Important as all these problems are, I remain convinced that the central issue concerns the role of the teacher, and in particular the relationship between knowing children and teaching them. I believe that it is possible to begin to redefine that relationship, and to fix it within a context in which pupils are relatively autonomous, even within the decadent structure of existing educational institutions. And that still seems to me as good a place as any in which to start.

MICHAEL MACDONALD-ROSS

Acquiring and Testing Skills

What kind of skills are relevant in the world we see developing? What problems are posed by assuming radical changes in the present educational system? And more specifically, how can skills be acquired and tested in a deschooled society? The effort to clarify these issues will involve some extensive and perhaps unusual detours; so it is just as well to start at the most familiar point. We can agree that a skill is usable knowledge, and to have a skill is to have the capacity to do useful things. This straightforward definition forms the boundary of our investigation.

I *What can be done now*
During the last few decades we have come some way towards understanding the ways skills may be learnt. Before the Second World War there was almost no organized knowledge about training; now we begin to have a coherent body of techniques which deserves to be called a technology of training. This development is so important to any discussion about skills that it needs to be examined more closely.

For most of mankind's history only one way to learn skills has been possible: a young person sits beside an expert and copies, more or less formally, the actions he sees the expert perform. The master no doubt gives hints and rules and monitors the student's progress in a rough and ready sort of way. In due course the student is formally recognized as a skilled person in his own right. Perhaps the best known example of such training methods is the apprentice system which has existed in England and other countries for many hundreds of years. The system serves to regulate entry into crafts and trades, to maintain standards and to give the apprentice a skill which once upon a time assured him of a permanent place in the community. A less hallowed example is the 'sitting by Nellie' training often found on the shop floor in light manufacturing industries. These traditional methods provide a way of *perpetuating* existing skills, of transferring them from one generation to the next or from one person to another. If evolution in methodology takes place at all it takes place very slowly. The individual is not expected to be innovative in any real sense; the social situation does not require this. Of course, changes in style and taste do occur in products sold directly to the public but this usually does not entail fundamental changes in technology. Another important assumption is that the number of craftsmen remain roughly the same from one generation to the next; and if rapid growth in numbers were required these methods would not provide a sufficient basis.

We now live in a world where these assumptions no longer hold true. There have been changes in technology and in the structure of society during the course of a single lifetime the like of which could hardly have been imagined a century ago. Later we shall look more closely at this process of change; but first consider the problems of training large numbers of people in skills which did not previously exist.

During the second world war and afterwards, the invention of entirely novel military systems (radar, atomic weapons, etc) and the rapid improvement of existing weapons (for example, the succession of new aeroplanes) created a quite novel training problem: how do you train men in sufficient numbers for equipment that does not yet exist? For quite often it was the lack of trained men that delayed the introduction of new equipment onto the battle-field. The story of training technology is the story of how this problem was solved, and how the relevant ideas then diffused to form the basis of modern industrial training.

The development of a new piece of equipment poses quite straightforward problems. Someone must build it, someone must operate it, and someone must maintain it. So trained personnel must be able to perform *specified tasks*. And this allows the aims of training to be quite clearly stated, and once specified a training programme can develop these skills in a series of carefully designed stages. Readers familiar with the literature will know that this systematic approach to training uses 'task analysis', 'skills analysis', or 'behavioural objectives' to define the goals of training. All these methods rely upon one idea: the idea of defining what the learner can do after training that he could not do before. This implies that the learner's performance will be monitored, that test scores after the learning experience will be compared to baseline performance. Only if certain standards are reached is the process considered satisfactory; otherwise some remedial action must be taken.

So the testing of skills cannot be thought of separately from their acquisition. Both become part of an integrated training system, tied together by the objectives: can the learner achieve the agreed aims? Can he perform the specified tasks?

We also know a good deal about how to achieve the goals of training once they have been defined. One striking development has been the growth of simulation. Few are trained on the job these days, especially if the task is a complex one. Usually this involves the design of special training environments, the most extreme being full-scale simulations of the working environment. The most elaborate simulators are designed for man-machine interaction, for instance airline pilots or space crews, but the principle is quite widely applicable. Learning in a simulator is both safe and efficient: an optimal sequence of tasks can be presented to the student in a way that would never be possible on the job.

The advent of computers has enabled us to design simulators which are adaptive, responding to the student's needs. Performance is monitored automatically, and the level of difficulty and nature of the task is varied according to the learner's progress. Not only is this efficient, it is also more interesting for the student who is never presented with training schedules that are either too exacting or too easy. Such an adaptive system also ensures that all trainees actually reach the preset standards of performance before being let loose on the real job – a matter of some importance.

This leads us towards programmed instruction, in this context perhaps the most important of all post-war developments since it is so well suited to acquiring and testing skills. Whether presented in book or machine form programmes allow the learner to proceed at his own pace and make his own responses. In some cases the student can choose his own pathway through the material, though naturally the extent of this choice is limited by practical constraints.

These modern ideas are the first steps towards individual learning since the learning experience is to some extent tailored to individual needs. They also allow independent learning, that is, you can learn on your own if you wish. Such facilities are prerequisites for any deschooled system.

Another significant modern idea is (paradoxically) the avoidance of training. Since training is costly and time-consuming it is now standard practice to examine alternatives before any training system is designed. It may be simpler to redesign the job, so that less skilled people can do it; or it may pay to recruit men who are already trained. Or it may be possible to deskill a job by providing job aids of various kinds. Job aids vary from a simple check-list (to reduce the amount of data an individual must carry in his own brain) to a complex computer system with which the individual interacts. In some cases (space capsules, electric power stations, etc) it no longer makes sense to talk only of trained men. One must talk of man-machine systems performing the tasks; and the training of the man cannot be thought of separately from the design of the machine.

These ideas, and others, are welded together as a fairly coherent methodology, sometimes called, rather ambitiously, a technology of training. We have now reached the stage where, once the objectives of training are well-specified, they can be achieved. But we should note that these ideas are not yet universally understood or accepted. Although it is true that the hardware-based military-industrial complex uses training technology extensively, it would be a mistake to think that all sectors of our society were similarly well organized. In many areas of our public, social, and education services, skills are still acquired haphazardly by old-fashioned methods. To illustrate this I shall discuss the skill of car driving, since it is familiar to most of us. But almost any example from the public sector could have been used to show fundamental deficiencies in training method.

Car driving is a particularly interesting case, since the rules for awarding licences in Britain are laid down publicly by the Department of the Environment and so presumably represent the 'best advice that is available to the Minister'. The central problem is this: most of those who pass the test are quite poor drivers – yet we know enough to ensure that virtually everyone could learn to drive well. How does this situation arise, and how can it be remedied?

In the first place there are some obvious anomalies, for example, the recitation of the Highway Code. Now in real life correct road behaviour is, in part, determined by correct responses to road signs and rules. It involves *attention* (signs must be noticed), *discrimination* (signs must be correctly and distinctly interpreted), and *action* (the driver's consequent behaviour must be appropriate). But in no sense at all is correct road behaviour dependant on a parrot-like ability at verbal recitation which is the way the Highway Code is tested. Obviously behind this system lies an implicit hypothesis that verbal performance transfers to live psychomotor performance, that is, because a driver can *say* the rules he will act in accordance with them. Both common sense and research evidence suggest that this sort of assumption is rarely borne out in practice.

Another well-known anomaly concerns motorway driving. Learners are not allowed on British motorways, yet when they pass the test they now have access to motorways, though quite untrained for this very special type of driving. The solution to this problem does not lie in allowing learners to practise on the motorway, as some have unwisely suggested. This would simply compound the error; for motorways (which are the safest of roads for skilled drivers) are the deadliest of environments for the learner, since the penalty for any mistake can be death. We need a way for learners to make their mistakes, and be corrected safely: that surely means some kind of simulation.

This gives the key to much of what is wrong with driver training and testing – too much of it takes place on the roads. Roads are now crowded and dangerous places, where critical decisions follow one another unceasingly. Learners are more than a nuisance to other drivers, they are a hazard. But the principal reason for criticising road training is that it is so inefficient and ineffective, whereas a properly designed simulator would be able to radically improve the standard of driving. I say this with complete confidence (though I am aware that existing car simulators are much less than optimal) because we already have the example of training airline pilots and spacemen by simulation. Who would ever dream of training them on

65

the job? Simulation can present all the key situations in proper sequence tailored to the individual's needs, and the learner's performance can be monitored and recorded so he can know exactly how he is progressing. On the road you may never encounter with your instructor the very situations that cause accidents – that sort of omission cannot happen with a simulator.

In a similar way, official testing should be done in simulators. The advantages of maintaining real standards and passing only those who can really drive are quite obvious. And experienced drivers would have the incentive to return for upgrading and reduction of insurance premium. I should acknowledge, in passing, two possible objections to these proposals, neither of which really carries much weight. Firstly, it is obvious that, sooner or later, a learner must practise on a real road with a real car. Of course I know this – but the stress should be on later rather than sooner. Secondly, the initial design (hardware and software) of a good simulator would be costly – but not nearly so costly as the present system, with its wasteful road lessons and tests, its dependance on manpower (trainers and testers) and the deaths and accidents that result inevitably from poor training. The huge numbers learning to drive every day of the week would make the expenses of design well worth while. And we *do* know how to do it.

There are other aspects of driving that would need special consideration, for instance, personal interactions between driver and driver or between driver and pedestrian. There are quite a number of situations where a driver's behaviour depends upon his assessment of what another will do, and what the other person thinks of him. Consider, for instance, the familiar problem of crossing the road, or situations where one car or the other must give way. The training of drivers in these situations can also be improved by the application of modern behavioural science, though it would take us too far afield to discuss this in detail.

The main lesson to be learnt from this case history is that modern training techniques are not yet widely applied by the social and public services. The key ideas have been developed by military and commercial training establishments, but have not yet diffused through the rest of our society. This we must bear in mind when we consider a deschooled society: so far the most effective training is done in the most formal establishments.

II *Alternative futures*

Since training technology arose from the needs caused by rapid changes in military and industrial methods, we should be especially sensitive to the needs of the future. There is, as a matter of fact, quite an extensive body of expertise concerned with forecasting the long-term future and with the question of specifying alternative futures. For some strange reason this work is never referred to by writers of the deschooling group; but the main conclusion of the futurologists are of central importance to anyone wishing to change the nature of education, since the effects of education are so long lasting. In this article I can mention only one or two important topics.

Running throughout this work is a recurring theme, that skills will go out of date much more rapidly than hitherto. This can be expressed in various ways. For example, it is sometimes said that children born today can expect to have three (successive) professions during their lifetime. Alternatively, it is said that the main areas of future employment will lie in the service industries and in industries based on novel technologies – such as holograms or information science. These expectations are likely to be broadly correct: they may be wrong in detail, but they surely will reflect general trends.

A related theme is the accessibility of information. We can expect the results of pure and applied research to become more easily accessible with the growth of information systems based on computers and other technologies. This will lessen the burden of detail that an individual must master, but will raise instead the question of how best to use this accessible knowledge. To most observers the outdating of skills and the growth and accessibility of knowledge has obvious consequences. First, we are now training people for jobs that soon won't exist. For example, the printing trade still takes on apprentices and trains them in traditional methods – though computer typesetting is already a reality. This kind of misdirection of human potential is nothing short of scandalous, and is by no means confined to the trades union arena. A large part of the six years' basic training suffered by medical students is scarcely applicable to modern medical conditions, and inside a decade much of the detailed factual knowledge learnt will be worthless. Successive Royal Commissions on medical education have failed to get to grips with the fundamental problems; as knowledge has advanced medical training has simply grown more lengthy and in some ways less relevant. The result is that our society has too few physicians (and will have for many years to come), and they will be scarcely prepared for the changes they will face in the future.

These are strong comments, but by no means original. Most people conclude that provision must be made for learning new skills later in life, retraining or adult education being the obvious answer to these problems. But in my opinion the problem runs deeper than this. It raises the whole question of relevance.

The deschooling movement can be seen as a protest against established institutions. It is, however, more fruitful to characterise the whole movement as raising the question of relevance in education. Again and again protests have been made against the context and style of current education. These protests imply a search for more relevant kinds of education, a quest that we should all take part in. In a similar way we need to discuss what *kinds* of skills might be relevant; my suggestions are outlined below.

III *Metaskills*

The mechanic repairing a car, the accountant balancing books, the doctor diagnosing an illness: these are all complex skills which take a long time to learn properly. It is natural and significant that training concentrates on the observable act – what the man must *do* in given circumstances. But behind these detailed skills lies a deeper and more fundamental set of skills, which I call *metaskills* (meta- in the sense of sharing, action in common). Two distinctive features identify these metaskills. They have a wide domain of application, that is, they are not situation-specific, and they are prerequisites for the acquisition of most of the specific skills.

Two of these metaskills are quite familiar: basic literacy and elementary mathematics. The ability to read and express oneself in spoken and written language is the most fundamental and the

68

most typically human of all skills. So many jobs depend upon literacy that its importance would be assured even if there were no attendant cultural opportunities available to the literate person – which of course there are. This all seems so obvious that it is difficult to understand how some thinkers can seriously suggest that we are moving into a 'post-literate' society where information will be communicated 'audio-visually.' On the contrary, it is likely that literacy will become more rather than less important, at least in the forseeable future. It may be in the very long term that computer-aided text composition will affect some occupations; but I do not think this weakens the general point that communication in any complex society depends upon the use of spoken and written language, and these are skills that can be learnt.

The same is true of elementary mathematics. More and more occupations have some quantitative or logical component, and those who are unable to handle the simplest of mathematical concepts are going to have a difficult time. Fortunately the computer will be of some use, for routine calculation is certainly destined for machines in future. And in the long term computers may change the very nature of mathematics – so perhaps one had better add that understanding how best to use computers is also a highly relevant skill for the future. At any rate, I think we can accept the view that an ability to use concepts of mathematics operationally is a prerequisite for quite a number of more specialised skills.

To some extent these two metaskills are already taught in schools. Not taught very well, perhaps, and certainly incompletely since significant areas of linguistic and mathematical skills are wholly omitted from most syllabi. In a short essay I cannot substantiate every opinion in depth, but let me make the following point : any deschooled system would have to make serious efforts to enhance literacy and mathematics, and the objectives should be much more far-reaching than allowed by the present school system. We can and we should do much better, for valuable information is available, but little used. And I am not necessarily referring to such methods as ita and new maths. Instead I would point to the discrepancies between the way in which language and mathematics are used in the outside world and the way they are taught in school: that is the departure point for any revision attempted by a deschooled system.

But there are important metaskills which are never taught at all in our present educational system. Consider, for instance the nature of problem-solving – not just maths problems, but any sort of problem. Problem-solving is a characteristic human activity, something we do all the time. How strange that we should never be taught anything about it! Yet countless specialized skills (for instance, diagnosing a fault or designing a new product) depend upon this general ability to solve problems. What does it involve? The key idea is the problem-solving cycle, sometimes known as the systematic approach to problem-solving. The sequence starts with a problem or puzzle. How well is it defined? Do we know what would count as an answer? Half the battle in solving a problem may lie in finding the most fruitful way to state it.

Once the problem is stated correctly it may have solved itself. On the other hand it may appear so complex that a model of the situation must be built. A model is a representation of some real situation which retains the essential conceptual relationships, but which is sufficiently simplified to allow for the application of standard techniques. The hypothesis is, that if a strategy succeeds on the model, it will also succeed in the real world.

Usually there are a variety of possible options – different heuristics or strategies that could be used to solve the problem. So the next steps are to generate and evaluate these alternatives. Eventually one method is chosen. Now we need a plan, consisting of the sequence of operations we intend to carry out. Usually we define stages en route as sub-goals, and then identify the operations needed to get from one sub-goal to the next. Then we can carry out the operations and evaluate the results.

Of course, we may not get it right. This means we must recycle; but more specifically it means we must try to identify where we went wrong. In computer jargon, this is 'debugging the programme' – and this concept is appropriate, for the sequence of instructions for a computer is indeed a plan to solve a particular type of problem. To debug is to think constructively about how a mistake happened, and decide what should be done about it. This contrasts vividly with the sort of attitudes most children get from present-day teaching – 'it's right' or 'it's wrong' – a hopelessly inadequate style of thinking. Some concepts cannot be grasped all at once, many problems cannot be solved at the first attempt. The right vs. wrong dichotomy prevents progress in such situations, and leads to mistaken ideas about the problem ('too hard) or about oneself ('I'm stupid').

Another interesting skill concerns personal interaction in groups [about which John Hipkin writes elsewhere in this book – Ed.]. Almost everyone's working life is spent as a member of some group, and often a whole set of groups. How should individual members of a team behave so that the team as a whole achieves its objectives? This is the question, and there is now a certain amount of knowledge that is relevant, certainly enough to design appropriate training courses.

Although experiments in teaching problem-solving and group dynamics do exist and have had some success, it would be idle to pretend that we know all there is to know, or that there already exist completely satisfactory procedures for acquiring and testing metaskills. The truth is that their importance is only just being realized, and it will be some time before suitable learning facilities could be made generally available. But by putting some resources *here* instead of on other less central aspects of education and training, we could make radical improvements in the ability of the student to learn for himself and to adapt to his continually changing job skills.

To sum up, metaskills are relevant because they have wide applicability and form the foundations of more specific skills. The success of retraining efforts later in life will largely depend on the extent to which a person has previously acquired these metaskills. In general they are not taught at all effectively by the existing school system, but they should play a major part in any deschooling programme.

IV *Training in a deschooled society*

First of all, we had better be clear what is meant by 'deschooling'. If it means just the abolition of compulsory school education I don't think the learning of skills will be greatly affected since so much training is done by technical colleges, companies and industrial training boards. But if it means the deinstitutionalization of all learning, well, that is a radical proposal. I shall assume we are dealing with the latter intention if only because it is more interesting for our purposes.

Training in skills presents a severe problem to deschoolers, which I do not think they have yet seriously faced. As we have seen, the most effective job training is done in the most formal establishments – the armed forces and the large industrial corporations. An implication is that the disestablishment of training would result in a widespread drop in standards. Is this inevitable? Can we envisage a course of action that would deinstitutionalize learning and still supply society with all the trained people that are needed? This the reader must judge for himself, though I can outline some of the key issues.

Why are formal organizations so effective at training in skills? Partly I suppose, because they face some fairly acute problems that must be solved. That is certainly why so many innovations have started in military systems. But large organizations also possess the *resources* to do a good job. They have the money, they have the capacity to take decisions and make them stick, and they can pursue forward policies more consistently than smaller groups. Make no mistake about it, the development of skills requires resources: time, expertise, hardware, software – these must all be available or we are back to square one with the apprentice system. So any satisfactory system must enable us still to allocate sufficient resources or people simply will not have the option of exercising choice.

A further difficulty is that the specialized skills are not needed by everyone – individual need and ability must be matched to the provision of resources. This is another difficulty with the deschooling position, which quite rightly aims to provide more options for the individual. But this presupposes a really sophisticated counselling system whereby people could identify their strengths (and weaknesses) in sufficient detail to help them make the best choices. We do not have such facilities available now, and their creation would require large central investments.

At least one of the problems of deschooling we can evade by revealing it as a pseudo-problem. Some deschoolers believe there is a 'who shall decide' problem – namely, who decides what people will learn. I must say I think this is an ill-formulated problem, if it is problem at all. It is not the case even today that control of the educational system is vested in any one individual or group, in some simple authoritarian hierarchy. Rather the reverse is the case: decisions happen by default because no one knows what to do, nor has the power to make decisions. But there are ways of improving decision-making capacity of social organizations which could be used with advantage in a deschooled society. For a start it is necessary to recognize that the centre of control will shift from place to place according to need – this is the concept of 'redundancy of command'. Next, the inevitability of conflict must be recognized, and conflict-resolution machinery must be designed for the situations which arise. In such a society 'who shall decide' could never be given a fixed answer.

Then there is the question of testing and certification. Since we have already agreed that testing is an integral part of the learning process this issue reduces to the question whether there should be a system of public certification in a deschooled society. It is all very well to say 'abolish exams'. I, too, think the effect of examinations on the educational system is generally pernicious, and certification has always been used to restrict entry to the professions and trades union. But the system does ensure some minimal standards. Would you like to be operated on by an uncertificated brain surgeon...? I suspect not. And though this may be an extreme example, quite a lot of jobs are 'vital' in the sense that, done wrongly, calamity can result. So the question becomes, how should performance be assessed and *to whom* should the results be available?

These stumbling-blocks must be recognized; but there is also a bright side to the picture. The development of techniques for individualized and independent learning are important in themselves, and are quite essential pre-requisites for acquiring skills in a deschooled situation. One of the reasons we have been stuck with such rigid institutions is, as we all know, the sheer logistics of face-to-face instruction. This constraint we can now demolish once and for all. In addition we should note the various technological developments which will allow students to operate from their own homes (for instance, multi-channel cable TV, two-way home communication sets, etc). This is the sort of technology that can free us from the logistic necessity of acquiring skills only in formal training establishments.

The idea of metaskills also provides hope – the hope of providing a sound foundation on which the individual person can later build his specialized expertise. I must confess I do not know whether metaskills could be learnt well in a deschooled system, but they are an answer to what I take to be the central message of the deschoolers – the plea for relevance. At any rate we could scarcely do worse than we are doing at present, and might well do a lot better.

ALISON TRUEFITT AND PETER NEWELL

Abolishing the Curriculum and Learning Without Exams

Curriculum implies the right of some to prescribe what others shall learn.

'What should be taught? ... Up to the age of sixteen nobody should go without some practical work, some experience in mathematics and some in humanities. And it ought to be a sizeable share of each. ... Up to this point we are rigorists. ... We would like to prescribe this for all pupils in all secondary schools as an obligation.'

Thus the Newsom Committee Report (*Half our Future,* commissioned by the British Ministry of Education and published in 1963) expressed a view which despite a great deal of tinkering in the name of 'curriculum reform' or 'curriculum innovation' is still almost universal.

If curriculum and its inevitable corollary, examinations, are to be abolished, two things must be demolished: the phoney epistemology that has buttressed them both all these years, and the whole exploitative social hierarchy which the curriculum-exam straightjacket serves.

First the epistemology. Curriculum and exams are possible because of the mistaken belief that knowledge is a *commodity* acquired by learning. The exam-curriculum system is constructed – ostensibly, that is – in terms of the three alleged elements in the process: knowledge, society, and the learner. Different philosophies place the stress differently.

The most dangerous starts from an inflated concept of knowledge. It is conceived as an almost mystical entity of permanent and universal value to mankind; something that exists in its own right like the life hereafter. As such it is a source of privilege and superiority – often described as 'excellence' – for its possessors.

'These and related qualities of mind in which we are interested have only become possible to us through the progressive elaboration of complex linguistic structures, social institutions, and traditions, built up over thousands of years. And they are

75

open to each child individually only by mastery of the complex non-natural world in which they are embedded. The abstract nature and complex structure of these objectives is such that the only way it would seem possible for youngsters to acquire these efficiently and effectively, is for us to introduce pupils to them deliberately and systematically.'

Thus P. H. Hirst and R. S. Peters, in *The Logic of Education,* express a curriculum rationale very commonly advocated by academics. Despite a flimsy attempt to find a source of curriculum nearer the hearts of individual learners – in 'public modes of experience' which they claim must determine the form if not the content of all human knowledge – they, and most educationalists, still believe that the reasons for learning lie outside the learner. Its form and content are therefore legitimately prescribed not *by* learners, but *for* them.

Professor Jerome Bruner agrees. 'Those who know a subject most deeply know best the great and simple structuring ideas in terms of which instruction must proceed' (*Revolution in Teaching*). Peters and Hirst put it this way: 'As in the case of curricular objectives and curricular organization, the point is that ultimately the decision, in all these cases, must rest necessarily in other hands, namely those of the teacher'.

This internal justification of curriculum in terms of knowledge, as opposed to more easily definable social or individual gains, leads to much disagreement about precisely how subject disciplines are to be derived from the main body of knowledge, and which subjects are, in any case, desirable. Traditional studies, in which time has allowed the number of authorities to accumulate – Latin, Greek, Ancient History, Pythagorean Geometry, Euclidian Algebra, the Renaissance, the Great Classics – therefore tend to be favoured. Like the emperor's new clothes, they are supposed to have a value which anyone with enough intelligence can appreciate.

So many of us have come under the spell of this view at one time or another that it is a hard one to shake. Even Ivan Illich suggests (*Deschooling Society*, Ch. 6) that the 'great classics' ought to mark a 'new turn in a person's life', instead of just being 'part of sophomore year'. But while one may say, reasonably, that such and such a book marked a turning point for oneself, or for a thousand or a million others, to suggest that this is

what the book *does* indiscriminately to everyone, is to make
no less of a veiled prescription than the teacher who tells a new
boy 'In this school children are well-behaved'.

More straightforward is the account of curriculum in terms
of society's needs. Surely, the argument runs (gaining force
daily as society becomes more centralized and owes more and
more to technology), we must teach technology, maths, Chinese
etc etc if we are to have the trained personnel needed to maintain and develop our present level of civilization. And we must
make sure that all members of society have a basic minimum
standard of literacy and numeracy. And we must tighten up
our exam systems so they really do guarantee to society the
skills it needs.

This view also has its own special, practical difficulties. Those
who share it – mostly politicians and business men – have not
yet quite won the day against those who regard knowledge as
the source of curriculum – mostly academics. The result is that
only some of the new disciplines allegedly needed by society
today – computer science, commerce etc – have found their way
into the old 'classical' curriculum which is still, in most
secondary schools, largely unchanged. Moreover the exam system is mainly in the hands of the academics and out of line
with the needs of employers.

On top of this the exam system is still being used to serve the
ulterior as well as the immediate aims of the curriculum.
People will not knowingly submit to being unjustly labelled. So
curricula and exams are constructed to perpetuate the myth of
equal educational opportunity. The Department of Education
(for England and Wales) continues to applaud schools which
issue 'certificates of endeavour' to 'non-academic' schoolleavers; and produced (in *Report on Education* No. 73) this
masterpiece of doublethink: 'Some areas have adapted the idea
of courses for non-examination pupils with a view to enabling
pupils to leave with some form of qualification'.

It is also worth noting, so far as the social defence of the
curriculum is concerned, that it implies that large-scale manpower forecasting and manipulation are both legitimate and
possible, though there is little evidence, as yet, to suggest either.
Rows of empty places in the science faculties of the world's
universities testify, already, to the difficulty of persuading

independent young people to study something which appears to them unconnected to their own real needs, what with the Bomb, and pollution, and their general feeling of alienation. However, these real needs are going to have to be very resilient if they are to stand up to the 'needs' of a society in which the interests of monopoly capital have taken full control of the curriculum.

The third species of curriculum argument, the argument in terms of the needs of individual learners, is the newest and the most hypocritical. The child-centred theories, which are supposed to put learners' autonomy first, are, as Peters and Hirst triumphantly show, no real threat to the curriculum. No reputable application of the theory seriously suggests that learners should be autonomous in relation to the curriculum – only within it.

'If however a student is reluctant to use materials accompanied by exercises the Skill Cards need not be used until he feels more comfortable with the program' generously offers the Teacher's Handbook in one of the recent Science Research Associates' *Dimensions* series. A new Integrated Studies project created by the official England and Wales Schools Council is designed 'to increase individual pupils' power to decide and pursue their own learning paths'. But is is nevertheless a curriculum, with pre-packaged materials and a course plan aimed at getting specific learning results, as, for example, 'to make pupils more aware of Man's need to communicate with his fellows'.

Child-centred theorists are correct in realizing that freedom is the learners' real need. But they do not believe that it is a need compatible with learning, and offer only negligible tokens to meet it. The closeness of their techniques to those of hardsell advertisers is no coincidence. Both share the desire to interest numbers of people in what they might not otherwise choose.

Real learning, as any pre-school child will demonstrate, is a process in which each individual creates his own unique 'curriculum'. He asks and seeks answers to the questions raised for him by his own unique experience. One could no more prescribe a set of answers to match all the different needs and experiences of every individual than one could design a single garment to fit them all.

The will to learn is synonymous with the basic human desire to gain understanding, and hence a chance to relate coherently to the environment – the environment meaning the sum of human experience, the physical world, the world of mind and of other people. To argue, as Hirst and Peters do, that this basic human interest cannot be a sufficient criterion of what is educationally valuable to the learner, is to make arrogant and unjustified judgements about other people's reactions, needs, and values. How does Peters know that 'blowing up frogs with bicycle pumps' (the example he gives) is 'educationally undesirable'? Who is he to say that it is less desirable than, for example, the common practice of dissecting the poor frog?

And how, similarly, can curriculum experts be sure (as they are) that left to their own devices children would learn sexual perversion, murder, and immorality? There is little evidence to suggest that the careful guiding of interests by means of the curriculum has kept society free from psychopaths – rather the contrary. At least it is interesting to note that even curriculum experts believe that people *can* learn unaided.

The mistrust of self-directed learning (which alone is capable of prodigious feats – no curriculum ever led Einstein to Relativity) owes more to a fear of mysterious mental processes than to evidence that people only learn under pressure. This is the final clue to the real function of the curriculum and exam system. The universal insistence on a 'good all-round' curriculum, the fear expressed even today in the most up-to-date Schools Council project that 'watch would need to be kept on balance and range so that a child is not over-developing one capacity' – this has nothing to do with the failure of self-directed learning. Quite the contrary. It is so potentially successful that curriculum must be introduced as a form of rationing to ensure a decent degree of conformity in human development.

Overall the engineering of conformity is, of course, the real aim of the curriculum-exam system. It is an instrument for sorting people into pre-determined channels, not according to their talents, or the superficial employment needs of society, but in order to maintain an economic and social pyramid in which privilege and influence are reserved for a very few.

This argument is a commonplace applied to school. It needs to be applied with, if anything, more force to the curriculum system. School you can blow up, close down, or at least make voluntary. But the intangible curriculum rat-race could – especially bereft of school's facade of equal opportunity, however sham – become even nastier and more oppressive than it is now.

As far back as 1964 Professor Harold Clark of Columbia University was estimating that more people in the USA were being educated in industry than in all public and private higher education institutions put together. Not even the most optimistic de-schooler would expect those industries to permit learning which could undermine their economic foundations. Since then, in the USA we have seen the beginnings of a payment-by results commercial curriculum enterprise which, though operating through the schools, might do so even more successfully outside them. We have, throughout the world, a growth of private 'crammers' whose sole aim is to get people through exams. And we have a growth in the out-of-school opportunities for certification – the correspondence or TV degree courses, the do-it-yourself programmed exam text. And in Philadelphia, one of the first faltering steps towards the de-schooled situation, the Parkway Project, which is without buildings and some other defining characteristics of school, is offering a curriculum of over one hundred courses which must nevertheless be taken according to a statutory pattern of credit requirements.

Teaching hard- and software have of course become big business in their own right. But something more than sheer profits may also have encouraged the growing tendency of corporations to diversify by entering the curriculum market, to appoint 'education officers', and sponsor educational research. It could be the sense of an impending vacuum to be left after the school system – which is now clearly in crisis – breaks down altogether. Already the English-speaking markets are flooded with curriculum materials produced after funding by Ford, by subsidiaries of giants like Rank-Xerox, IBM, Time-Life, RCA and so on. Smaller companies and government agencies are not slow to follow.

If school is dying, a new kind of curriculum monopoly is just round the corner: our reference libraries and materials will be prepared for us by the top computer firms; taped materials will be made and shown by the media monopolies; the drug consortia will handle the medical curriculum, oil and other science-based industry will be responsible for the science curriculum – including ecology and pollution; the publishers will teach literature, the printers art, and government agencies history and geography. Employment in any field will depend on passing the examination designed by the monopoly holder in that field, and access to materials will be similarly limited.

The moral of all this is that, though de-schooling may provide the necessary conditions for real learning, that will not be enough. Until we have a fairer social set-up, progress towards a genuinely de-schooled, non-curricular society might best be moderated by some sort of learning institutions – without, of course, the compulsory dehumanization associated with schools. In other words, it is essential to abolish curriculum before abolishing school, although it will be much more difficult and will take much longer.

Three steps are possible now in our exam-ridden scene. They could begin to eliminate the factors associated with curriculum and exams which now inhibit real learning.

First and foremost would be the removal of any compulsion to follow any form of learning prescription – from general 'all-round' curricula to particular programmed packages. (The experience of schools, like Summerhill, which do not practise compulsion, shows that a skill such as reading can be rapidly acquired if it is not the sole object of a rigid curriculum.) So far as learners want to answer their questions by reference to second-hand sources – books, tapes, etc – what is needed is an encyclopedia or dictionary or card-index system, from which they can build up their own 'textbooks' if they wish, and to which they could also contribute entries. In a less-than-ideal world one would expect such a system, which each learning-centre could build up for itself, to coexist with the garish little packages designed to meet this or that certification requirement. But it would have to be up to the learners alone to decide which to use and what use to make of either.

The second step, already begun in a few places, is to encourage organizations other than school to play a part in people's learning. This does not mean – as some would prefer – that school should expand still further to embrace a glimpse of local industry, a bit of community service, and a visit to the law courts.

81

On the contrary, it means that school begins to take a much diminished role – approaching that of the reference library or advice bureau – while other social organizations take over as unmediated sources of information about themselves.

The open 'learning society' is still a long way ahead, but that is no reason why we should not start campaigning to persuade these organizations – including the commercial giants whose curricula threaten our freedom – to offer work experience of their own plant, rather than materials indirectly selling their products; and to allow their employees to take time to answer questions about their work, rather than appointing a cover-up information officer to do the job at arm's length.

The third step is also planned as an antidote to the curriculum likely to be peddled out-of-school by corporations for their own ends, and to the alienation and sense of hopelessness which our present social system breeds. It would be an attempt to remove barriers to learning created by the fragmentation of families into impotent little nuclear units; by the implication built into the school system that unstructured learning is either impossible or second-rate; and by the withholding of information about the real workings of society without which coherent behaviour is impossible. This step is not likely to bear fruit if based on a learning institution, or other administrative set-up. Mediation by institutions of processes which ought to be individual, autonomous responses is the disease; the cure must be in terms of direct human contacts. In other words, we must take initiatives, talk to people, fight bureaucracies, and join in communities.

Beyond these steps it is harder to predict what form the fight should take. One thing is clear: it cannot be confined to the field of education as presently conceived. One of the aims of the de-schooling movement is to make possible the 'learning society', but that will only be achieved by fighting our present society at every point where it undermines the autonomy on which true learning depends.

One powerful tactic from within the educational field might be to formulate very clearly a rationale for curriculum and certification which should not be abused as an instrument of privilege. For although the curriculum must be abolished, and learning is only possible without exams, certification is, for some purposes, essential. If these purposes can be defined beyond all doubt, it will be more difficult for society to confuse them with learning.

The definition will, ultimately, be a definition of autonomy. It is right, surely, in cases where individuals have for some reason to relinquish their autonomy, that they should receive some guarantee that those to whom they have handed responsibility are competent to take it. Autonomy is, as ever, the key. When a man will have to be unconscious during an operation, when he puts his life into the hands of an airline pilot, he is entitled to assurances about the competence of the doctor or the pilot. This is not to say that either must have followed specific curricula or passed standard tests. Neither possibility is ruled out. But the essential point is that they be competent to carry out the wishes of those for whom they've taken responsibility. Only their performance in this task must be guaranteed: appendix removal, not O Level Latin; piloting, not Shakespeare recitation. Moreoever the patient or passenger has a right to name his required guarantee. He cannot insist, but he can refuse to hand over responsibility if he is not satisfied.

A detailed look at the implications of this principle, including a realistic appraisal of the actual performances required of such 'responsible' people, would yield something rather less than the rationale for the compulsory, exam-ridden curriculum that is the backbone of the present school system.

JOHN HIPKIN

Learning in Groups

In the conventional classroom the teacher is intentionally didactic and directional. He takes charge of what goes on because he believes that the purpose of the lesson is to communicate to his pupils a specified amount of subject matter. He initiates and they respond; he talks and they listen; he judges and they are judged. Good pupils are defined as those who comply with the teacher's wishes; for those who deviate there are appropriate sanctions.

We are so used to 'talk and chalk' teaching that it is difficult to conceive of it in any other form. When we speak of 'the teacher' in this essay we mean quite simply anyone, however 'qualified', who can help others to learn. Usually, but not invariably, the most efficient teachers are likely to be those with special training and experience and with a deep interest in what they are doing. Learning in groups will certainly need skilful handling and we assume that it will be most effective when arranged and guided by teachers with developed confidence and understanding. None of this is intended to discount the great value of cooperative group learning where there is no formal teacher figure but where students learn from one another and 'teach' one another. Such groups often work very efficiently but in our view *most* systematic learning needs the particular help of a skilled and qualified teacher.

It would be wrong to suggest, however, that the only justification of group learning is that it helps to turn out pupils with better attitudes to learning. Another raison d'être is that it is the most effective mode of achieving certain kinds of objectives. If our aim is to help pupils understand human problems, for example, and if these problems entail a sensitivity to other people's opinions, an awareness of their situation and their motivations, then it is clearly of help to explore such problems with people who can extend the range of our experience and knowledge by offering their own. Indeed whenever a problem

84

is better elucidated by considering what people in their diversity have to offer, groups come into their own.

From what has already been said it is clear that group learning involves a distinct notion of what shall count as worth knowing: what do we need to know in order to explore a problem further? Pupils, teacher, neighbours, experts, documents etc, can all provide sources of knowledge for a study project, and it would be pedantic to insist that some sources prove more useful than others, or that the teacher might have told the group what they discovered for themselves only after laborious effort. Part of the justification of group learning is that pupils cultivate an understanding of *how* to learn effectively. Furthermore, if pupils pursue genuinely open-ended problems they will have to judge how to interpret a variety of considerations which can be of help in forming an opinion. Students are thus encouraged to construct their own world views; to take responsibility for how they choose to construe the world. This might be regarded as the highest aim of education.

Finally learning in groups is a more complex social activity than conventional classroom teaching. Patterns of interaction in the classroom are relatively straightforward – from teacher to pupil and back again – but in a group situation communications can go between any conceivable combination of group members. Because of this enormous complexity group learning is more difficult to handle or control and more of what is going on can go wrong, but conversely when a group gives its energies and resources to learning it can make great headway. In the remainder of this essay we shall consider how the learning objectives of a group are influenced positively and negatively by the dynamics of its social life.

For most teachers and students group learning is likely to be a new experience and one that contrasts very markedly with what they have grown used to in the conventional classroom situation. Many features of this new activity – the role of members, the physical arrangements, the use of learning resources etc – will be so bewildering that students and teachers may sense a good deal of insecurity, amounting at times to anxiety. There will often be a deep apprehension that too many factors in the learning situation are unfamiliar or unpredictable, that it is difficult to discern any purpose or form in what is going on and that it is impossible to assess the effectiveness of the whole enterprise. In this atmosphere of uncertainty and tension there may be a tendency for members to precipitate a 'showdown' in the hope that 'normality' can be restored. Students may become withdrawn and uncooperative, even hostile; the teacher may feel assertive and punitive. Teacher and pupils alike may 'conspire' to show that the whole idea was misconceived in the beginning and is unworkable. This 'conspiracy' theory may seem a little far-fetched in view of the fact that those teachers and pupils who experiment with group learning are likely to be the ones who are most anxious to get away from traditional patterns of authority and teaching. What is suggested here however, is that the choice is not always in terms of new methods or old but between feelings of security and insecurity. People find it difficult to innovate when they are frightened.

The task of rendering a group secure, of giving it a sense of optimism that its purposes will succeed, cannot be reduced to a simple formula: it is a complex operation involving a sensitivity to a wide range of group and individual characteristics. We shall consider some of these characteristics as variables likely to affect significantly the ability of a group to function effectively.

In a conventional classroom the teacher is an authority in two senses: he is in charge of the group because he largely controls its activities, but he is also in possession of the knowledge which counts. In a group learning situation he is not an authority in either of these senses, but becomes more a stimulus and a resource. He helps students to define and to achieve learning goals which they in part determine, and to which they feel committed. Students may initially regard this change of role with suspicion. They may charge the teacher with not doing what he is supposed to do, or more tellingly, paid to do. The teacher will need to take such charges seriously. He will need to ask himself whether he is not the unwitting victim of the 'conversion syndrome', which involves the total relinquishment of all former approaches in favour of a range of new and largely untried ones. Such a policy may cause him to 'lose his grip' and give rise to his students' unease. The teacher's task is to adopt new roles without cutting himself off from existing strengths, for he will certainly need all his professional experience and competence if he is to make the new methods acceptable and effective.

Another explanation of students' criticisms is that they may unconsciously wish to regain their dependent status upon the teacher. They may push him to reassume an authoritarian stance – not because they prefer being told what to do but because they will again know 'where they stand' and they will then be able to resume familiar postures such as unquestioning compliance or equally indiscriminate rebellion. Teachers may find these relationship tensions exhausting and complain that they spend too much of their time attempting to secure the degree of motivation, persistence and trust which are essential to learning. 'Whenever are we going to get down to it?' may become a cri de coeur. Viewed in this light the long period of preliminary negotiations about roles and procedures may well appear wasteful but it is precisely the failure of traditional methods to encourage students to take a full measure of responsibility for their own learning which has led to the adoptions of new approaches. To have secured some of the minimal conditions of self-directive learning is to have made enormous progress.

In these circumstances the teacher in school will need above all else to develop patience and understanding – not easily evolved qualities when the pressures for 'achievement' are so strong. He can be helped however by colleagues who share similar challenges or who are supportive of him in his new role; helped, too, by his students who should be encouraged to evolve learning aims which both they and their teacher value and to cooperate in their achievement. Teachers and students should spend time together asking such questions as: What are the blocks to learning? How do they arise? How can they be removed? Any teacher who finds himself isolated from his colleagues in the task of innovation or who cannot evolve aims which his students are willing to share is likely to suffer frustration and, perhaps, in the end, defeat.

The firmest point of orientation for a group is its task. A group should know what its task is and be committed to it. Nothing undermines the morale of a group so completely as a sense of its not getting anywhere. Thus the task will need at some point to be explicitly acknowledged. Merely to assume that it has been understood is to risk tipping the balance of the activity very much in favour of purely private goals, since in the absence of explicitness members will take the task to be what they are happiest to regard it as being. From time to time the teacher

87

may need to remind the group of what it has set out to do, and to judge in the light of their response whether he should persist with the task, amend, or even abandon it.

Getting a group to acknowledge and stick to a task is not easy. When a group of people sit down together—whether as students at a seminar, committee members, planners or whatever—they usually set out with an agenda, a statement of the ground to be covered, of the tasks to be handled. This is the public agenda in that it represents a shared view of what the group is there to do. But every group comprises individuals, each of whom has his own unique concerns and aspirations. One may be out to impress upon others that he is a man to be reckoned with. He may not give himself over to the task until his view of himself has been acknowledged by the group. Another may formally accept the task but privately consider it hopeless. By a process of subtle undermining he may seek to fulfil his own diagnosis. Still another may feel hostility against particular individuals or minorities within the group. Anyone who has ever attempted to work in a group has witnessed these private preoccupations overshadowing common goals. The group can only make progress against these negative influences if members are helped to see what is happening (either within the group setting or privately). The problem is to help dissident individuals to set their private agendas on one side for the sake of common objectives but this they will not do until they are acknowledged as individuals with value.

In the last analysis a group is held together by a shared commitment to certain group norms. There must be rules or conventions governing the conduct of the activity—understandings about how things are to be decided and acted upon. For example, people will be expected to show a kind of respect for others as demonstrated by punctuality, attentiveness and tolerance. If group members get the feeling that anything goes then in time nothing will go well.

Group norms should not however become so pervasive that they suffocate. A respect for the autonomy of a chairman may be essential, for example, but if the chairman assumes dictatorial powers then the group must check him. Similarly, courtesy and consideration are important but if they cloak genuine disagreement they become dysfunctional, in that they inhibit the very goals they are intended to help achieve.

The building up of this group spirit is of very great importance. It can be gauged by such questions as: What do group members experience when they return to the group from other activities? How do they anticipate this reunion? These general feelings about the group reflect its ethos or personality. Of course every one of the constituents of group behaviour go toward the making of an ethos but certain general considerations seem particularly important. Is the group open and cooperative, or exclusive and competitive? How does it view the 'outside'? With suspicion and hostility or with curiosity and confidence? Is the temper of the discussion such that everyone has a chance to contribute? What part does humour play in its life? How open and trusting are members of the group? These dispositions and norms support or weaken everything the group attempts to achieve.

A group cannot function until the problem of leadership is faced. A teacher has to renounce authoritarian postures and to invite his students to take a greater measure of responsibility for their own learning without giving the impression that no one is finally responsible for the conduct of the activity. What gives the teacher his special status is that he is seeking to renounce his authority so that others can assume it. He does not achieve this by appearing to wash his hands of responsibility for what happens to the group. Leadership does not, of course, entail telling other people what to do. Rather it involves giving people a sense of their potentialities and offering them ways in which these might be realized. Teachers should be ideally qualified to lead in this sense but students can lead too. They will not exercise leadership functions responsibly unless they are invited to do so. In the absence of such an invitation they may exercise them irresponsibly.

The size, composition, and arrangement of a group all have a marked bearing upon how well it functions. It is not possible to prescribe an ideal group size since so much depends upon the nature of particular tasks, the composition of the group, its level of maturity, etc. The best criterion of group size is therefore an empirical one. Signs of an overlarge group are that breakaway groups begin to form, factions develop, and people address the group as though it were an audience. It is too small if people feel on top of one another, under too close scrutiny, or compelled to participate when they would rather reflect. Discussion groups are usually too small with under seven members and too large with over fifteen.

A group's membership can comprise people differentiated by sex, age, status, race, religion and a host of other traits. When composing a group it is very important to consider how these membership variables are likely to affect the group's behaviour. If for example a discussion group is made up of students normally taught in different ability sets, or of employees drawn from different levels of the occupation hierarchy, it may be difficult to get discussion of issues concerned with authority, power, or social justice. Indeed it may be difficult to get any discussion at all, especially if those from lower status groups are in a minority. The same sort of considerations apply when tackling subjects like sex, with coeducational classes, or race, with ethnically mixed groups. It is surprising how often discussion group leaders blame poorly motivated groups for failures which are basically due to an unwise choice of membership or task. As a solution to this problem some teachers see great merit in friendship-groupings – pupils working with chosen friends. Such an arrangement has many superficial attractions – pupils seem better motivated, cooperation between them is easier to achieve and the problem of group composition is simplified. Nevertheless there are dangers. We know from sociometric studies that friendship groupings reveal 'isolates', that divisions are made on the basis of sex, ability, social class, ethnic origin etc. If an activity requires diversity and the extension of understanding of how other people think and feel then friendship groupings may be inimical to these ends. Friendship groupings may also result in a kind of collusion, a concerted resolve 'to work to rule', or 'not to get out of line'. Finally, the considerations which make friends valuable in the playground may not do so in the classroom. A boy who enjoys playing football with his mates may welcome the opportunity in school to work with different people who stimulate him intellectually.

In setting up a group – its size, shape, formation etc – a group leader needs to be particularly conscious of his own position within it. Does it signal the kind of status which he is anxious to assume? Is his chair larger, more formal than theirs? Is he in any sense noticeably apart from the group? Is he in front of a blackboard or behind a desk? Where are students placed in relation to him? Do those who seek to please him try to sit near him? Are the 'rebels' seated together? Do boys and girls face one another across a chasm? Shape too is important. Is the group ragged (some inside, some outside)? Can people see one another? Are people more comfortable sitting behind a table or circle of desks or would they prefer to sit in easy chairs facing one another? Each of these considerations can affect a group's preparedness and ability to get down to the task.

It is sometimes imagined that groups are self-sufficient. In very few cases is this true. Most groups need input – data, evidence, stimulus or information upon which to exercise themselves. Understanding, for example, does not develop in a vacuum but in relation to specified problems and in the light of available data. Input must not be allowed to swamp the group however – it must be able to exercise discrimination and judgement if it is to function as a group.

One notable example of group learning in British secondary schools is that of the Humanities Curriculum Project, which sets out to help adolescents understand a wide range of human problems and of the value issues they raise. In these discussions the teacher acts the role of a neutral chairman in that he does not seek to promote his own point of view. The discussion is 'fed' with evidence on tape, film, photographs or written extracts from literature, journalism etc and then discussed. What pupils make of the evidence is up to them since it cannot of itself supply definitive answers to human problems. In this situation knowledge is a resource available to learners who are defining their own interests and concerns.

How is one to assess how effectively a group is learning? Whether it is attaining its objectives? The problem of assessment or evaluation is particularly difficult since so much group work pursues intangible or 'subjective' objectives. Perhaps the most important shift in the perception of what assessment entails is from the attempt to measure *attainment* (What do my students know now that they didn't know when they started the course?) to the diagnosis of *process* (How effectively are my students setting about the task of learning?). The difference between these two questions is important. A group leader with an attainment model in mind will be inclined to use the group as a teaching vehicle, and he will reward students according to

91

what they have learned. Students will resume dependency relationships upon the teacher since he sets the standards and hands out the rewards and penalties. They will spend energy and time trying to guess what is on the teachers' mind – what he is after, since he decides who succeeds and who fails. The *process* model, by contrast, regards student involvement in the evaluation as an important learning activity in itself. Students and teachers generate standards which they respect and pursue, and they discuss together the problems and difficulties which these standards present.

Some teachers, however, will find themselves forced by circumstances to assess students' group work in the sense of having to judge their attainment. It seems to be especially important in this connection that the teacher should exempt the discussion process from assessment. If students suspect that they are 'on trial' or 'under surveillance' they may 'perform' or withdraw so that their behaviour may become fashioned by the very process which is designed to evaluate it. Evaluation should act as a stimulus to learning, not inhibit it.

All that we have so far said about learning in groups assumes it is taking place in schools. This is not the impression I wish to give. In dwelling upon this aspect I have not sought to endorse schooling as such or to undervalue alternative structures of education. Indeed, in many ways, I have sympathy with those who believe schools to be obsolete institutions. I cannot however envisage in the foreseeable future any alternative means of providing popular education in a society as complex as ours. What needs urgently to be done is to strip schools of much of their formalism and artificiality. The chasm between life and learning may hasten the movement toward genuine community children. The school must therefore become more closely integrated with the wider community; indeed it should be a source of revitalization in many of our sterile neighbourhoods. Group learning may hasten the movement toward genuine community schools because it is a mode of learning which ascribes value to the experience of the learner, which works best in relation to the understanding of human problems, and which benefits from data from a wide range of authentic sources. As a mode of learning it entails a quality of social interaction which I believe to be essential to the survival of humane values in education.

ALBERT HUNT

Improvisation with Adults

It is a generally agreed educational principle that young children learn through play. It is also generally assumed that at a certain age people stop learning through play, and have to be taught in a much more formal way.

For the past few years I have been working with young adults – mainly in art colleges – in situations where we have been learning together through play. In this chapter I want to describe some of this work and then try and examine some of its more general implications.

I first began working in games situations in Shrewsbury some years ago, when I was asked to produce a play by John Arden and Margaretta d'Arcy, *Ars Longa, Vita Brevis*. The play takes a sharp child's eye view of the absurdity of schools and teachers. It opens with a Speech Day and a Headmaster's report: 'It has been a very good year, and we have all made a lot of money.' The Headmaster announces the appointment of a new art master; the art master turns a drawing lesson into a military drill, which ends in a battle. He is sacked and joins the territorial army. While he is out on Sunday manoeuvres in the woods, he is shot by the Headmaster, who is hunting with the Governors ('Shooting animals is much more pleasant than going to church on a Sunday'). His widow enjoys herself with young men in fast cars.

The play not only takes a child's eye view of the world (for example, the opening speech-day ceremony is like an irreverent schoolboy's imitation of his pompous headmaster): it's also built up around children's games. And so it seemed logical to begin by playing games, as a rehearsal technique.

I'd recruited the group simply by inviting anybody who wanted to help make a play to come along. On the first Saturday morning, eight people turned up. (I've since discovered that to get the most out of this kind of activity, you need roughly eight to fifteen people: it's possible to work with less than eight, but with more than fifteen it becomes difficult

to do sustained work). At first I felt a bit inhibited about inviting eighteen and nineteen-year-old students to play games. We
began by throwing a ball about. I'd read up some games in the
scouting manual the night before, in case nobody could think
of anything to do.

I needn't have bothered. Within twenty minutes we were all
arguing about the rules of games we'd played as children.
Regional variations appeared, different uses of language. We
played leapfrog, games of tig, British bulldog – in which you
capture people by lifting them off the ground, and they have
to resist capture any way they can. We really played these
games. It wasn't like the 'games' at youth club socials, where
people play at playing. We all became totally involved, and
after several hours we were covered with scratches and bruises.
When we were exhausted, we sat round a tape-recorder and
played at making official speeches. Each person chose a particular character – an archbishop, a queen, a prime minister – and
a speech, consisting of a paragraph from a women's magazine,
to go with the character. The speeches were then intercut on to
tape at random – the choice of speaker at any given moment
being determined by a throw of dice.

Later, we put the verbal game and one of the physical games
together. There's a children's game in which one person stands
with his face to the wall at one end of the room, while the rest
try and creep up behind his back and try to touch him.
From time to time, he looks round, and sends back to the
starting point anyone he sees moving.

We turned this into a classroom situation. The 'teacher' was
giving an illustrated lesson, writing on a blackboard. Behind
the 'teacher's' back, the 'children' were trying to change places
with each other. If the 'teacher' turned round from the blackboard, and caught a 'child' moving, the child became the
teacher. But when they became 'teachers', the players took on
the roles they'd developed in the verbal game around the tape-
recorder. So it wasn't just any old teacher giving a lesson at the
blackboard. It was the Archbishop of Canterbury. Or the
Queen. Quoting, of course, from a women's magazine.

This game was eventually translated directly into a scene in
the play: the scene in which the art master teaches children
how to draw straight lines. In our version, the children, wearing

crude, identical masks of plain cardboard rectangles with round holes cut in for eyes, sat perfectly still and stared, unresponsive, at the art master. But each time he turned his back to arrange his triangles and cubes, they swiftly and silently changed the shape of the classroom. As he confronted the same, identical, motionless faces, sitting in different places, one felt that he had lost all grip on reality. It was a very funny but very frightening image – and it had been created out of a children's game.

The games we'd played in the *Ars Longa* rehearsals had been consciously shaped towards the performance of a text. But as we played we quickly came to realize that the games had a validity in their own right. In the first place, they were physically liberating. We found ourselves using our bodies in ways that, as adults, we hadn't used them for a long time. And our physical responses to each other, in working situations, became instinctive, in the way that footballers in a good team respond instinctively to each other. And the change in response wasn't only physical. Paradoxically, the game structure had allowed us to behave much more naturally and openly with each other. We had discovered things about ourselves and about each other that we would not have discovered without the games. Discussions in the group became concrete and meaningful, because we were operating in a context that we'd created, and not in a realm of abstract argument.

Moreover, it had become clear that some of the games were capable of being developed into complex dramatic experiences in their own right. And so, with another group of students, this time in Bradford, after playing a number of games, simply for the sake of releasing a lot of energy and creating a group relationship, I suggested that we should take one of the games and turn it into an event that could be presented as a performance.

We began with a simple blindfold game. Two players wore blindfolds. The first player was looking for a shoe that we'd placed in the playing area: the second player was trying to find the first player before the first player found the shoe.

Even in this simple form, the game is more dramatic to watch than most conventional theatre. Played with concentration, accidental tensions and patterns and ironies develop. Players reveal their characters and ways of thinking in most unexpected ways: some work swiftly and feverishly, other stand still and listen. You can *see* a non-verbal intelligence at work. It's vital that the spectators should sit completely still and silent, so that the concentration isn't disturbed. (Incidentally, whenever we play games, one or two players take it in turns to watch and learn from the behaviour of the others).

We took the simple form and began to develop it. The aim we set ourselves was to create a game that would be self-explanatory to spectators. So at each step we invited people from outside the group to come and watch, and asked them to describe to us what they thought was happening. If the description was confused, we refined the game accordingly.

First we added two extra players. Then we changed the blindfolds into tall, stiff paper bags from a greengrocer's. The paper bags gave the players a strange, non-human appearance. Then we gave the players flags, two red and two blue, to distinguish them. We added more players and gave them flags too. At this point, the search for the shoe became meaningless: and so, instead, we made one man the hunter. He was armed with a blue flag *and* a stick, and had the right to 'kill' anybody he caught. He was only supposed to kill the reds – but since he couldn't distinguish red from blue, he tended to kill as many of his friends as of his enemies. A referee, who could see, and who dressed himself in a top hat and frock coat and controlled the game with a whistle, kept the score, by pricking balloons, red or blue, which were attached to the side of the stage. He laid the bodies, still clutching their flags, in heaps at the front of the stage. To make the game more difficult and more interesting, the students had devised a mobile structure on the stage. Hanging from the ceiling were two cross-beams, from which, in turn, hung old tyres, tin cans with stones that rattled, dummies, polythene bags and other old junk. If anyone collided with these objects, the whole structure whirled round, so that the environment in which the blindfold players were moving was constantly changing. Tension was added by the fact that the stage was about four feet high: players were always in danger of falling off. In the end, we created, from this blindfold game, a complex performance that held an audience's attention for twenty-five minutes. Afterwards, we would invite the audience themselves to play.

What had we learnt from this experience? Firstly, we had learnt, again, to work together as a group. Secondly, we had extended areas of physical experience, learning to move without eyes through a changing environment, feeling textures without seeing them. Thirdly, since we made the event for an audience, we'd been forced to ask ourselves fundamental questions about communication, clarity, entertainment.

But, above all, we'd learnt that it was possible to work in a serious, involved way by *playing*. The play had created its own discipline – but the discipline was enjoyable. The final results, after five days' work with twelve people, were on a level which would have been impossible in a conventional classroom situation.

Both the pieces of work I've described were ultimately involved with performance. But it seemed to me, in analysing the work, that the essential theatricality of play could be used in learning situations not directly concerned with performance. The theatre we had done was concrete and physical. The first, important step, therefore, was to create concrete, physical situations, potentially dramatic in themselves, so that students could learn by experiencing, rather than by listening to other people's experiences. And so, as the centre of the liberal studies programme at Bradford Art College, we invented a programme of fortnightly projects, loosely built around the idea of dramatic situations. We asked every student to take part in at least one of the projects, but left the choice to the individual student, since the element of personal commitment was central. We hoped, by the sheer variety of the programme, to offer something for everybody.

From a dramatic point of view, these projects fell roughly into two types. There were those in which the students went outside college, and became involved with the local environment; and there were others in which students stayed in the studio, but invented the outside world, through play and improvisation.

In most of the environmental projects, the basic, theatrical prop was a tape-recorder (to which, more recently, we've added a portable video-camera). A tape-recorder is, in itself, a play element: a conversation across one becomes a simple, and agreeable, social game. The machine structures and formalises the relationship. (For example, an unemployed school-leaver would never dream of going up to a complete stranger in the street, announcing that he's unemployed, and asking what the stranger thinks about it : given a video-camera, he'll do just that. Again, schoolchildren, given video equipment and told to do what they like with it, turn on an endless series of improvisations, which they'd never invent without the camera and monitor.)

At the simplest level, a student recording an old man who fought in the First World War, or a group of Hell's Angels, or a woman in a council house describing how Jesus has healed her of multiple sclerosis, or a miner describing his job, or a former navigator in a plane that bombed Dresden describing *his* job, or an eighty-two year old footballer talking about the 1914 cup final, or a Pakistani bus-conductor talking about Bradford ... is involved in a dramatic situation. If the student edits the First World War tape, and plays it back as part of a longer tape to a group in the British Legion club on Armistice night; or plays the tape of Midlands Hell's Angels to a Hell's Angels group in Bradford; or allows, accidentally, the former navigator to see pictures of the children's bodies piled up in Dresden: then the dramatic experience becomes much more complex. The initial situation is only a starting-point, but an essential one.

The projects in the theatre studio have been mainly extensions of, and developments from, the *Ars Longa* and blindfold projects. For example, basic game situations are extended into improvisations. A father sits waiting for his daughter. He's told her to be in by eleven, and now it's half-past three. When the daughter arrives, she has to talk herself across the room and out through the bedroom door. If she succeeds, she wins the game. Again, a young man arrives home at his flat late one night to find the door locked, as usual, but inside a totally strange girl sitting watching his television. The girl has to explain what she's doing there. If she succeeds in convincing the young man that it's really her flat, she's won. And again, a policeman comes to your door and asks you to go down to the police station. He won't tell you what you're wanted for. If he succeeds in persuading you to go, he's won. (A variation on these domestic games is to have them played by film stars: thus, John Wayne is the angry father, Marlene Dietrich the daughter ...).

None of these improvisations is intended for performance (in fact, I always discourage 'acting', unless it's an obvious caricature like John Wayne, and ask simply to work at exploring the situations). But it's possible to make the situations themselves much tougher. So: the question is asked – 'Are there any situations in which you would be prepared consciously to torture someone?' The conventional answer is, 'No.' And so the object of the group is to invent situations in which torture is apparently unavoidable. (One of the aims of this kind of improvisation is to offer a dialectical experience: the girl has to argue from the angry father's point of view; the radical student becomes a policeman; the liberal is placed in the position where he has to order torture.)

Another development of the game situation has been in a more obviously intellectual direction. So a group took George Orwell's *1984*, and from it invented Newspeak (they published a Newspeak magazine). Another group invented a religion and the rituals to go with it. The only rule was that the religion had to be at least as plausible as any of the established religions. (One student invented the self-imprisoning God, a being consisting of nuclear energy, who had imprisoned himself in matter, and then invented man so that man should evolve until he was able to release – nuclear energy. This seems to me at least as sensible as the self-sacrificing God of Pauline theology.) Yet a third group created an alien intelligence. Since the idea of an alien intelligence is, by definition, outside our range, they did it by writing on pieces of paper various imaginary attributes of an intelligence, and picking five of them out of a hat. They analysed a number of films, including *High Noon*, from the point of view of this intelligence (in this they were joined by the Orwell group, who produced a critique in Newspeak). Both groups learnt, incidentally, a lot about how the way films are read is conditioned by the assumptions the spectator brings to the film.

A third extension of the idea of games has been towards the role-playing situation – but this has also taken on visual and dramatic elements not normally associated with simulation exercises. The most successful example of this was a Vietnam War Game, in which a group played out an imaginary blockade of Hanoi. But they did so by setting up their various headquarters in studios and workshops all over the college, by wearing very clear visual symbols, and by placarding the college with rival posters. The result was that large numbers of students not taking part in the game became involved: a spontaneous Committee of 100 was formed, and a student took over the role of Bertrand Russell. (The negotiators always threw Russell's statements into the waste-paper basket. When the crisis was over, Russell put out a pamphlet saying that once again he had saved the peace of the world. They threw that into the waste-paper basket, too.) Since then, we have played an unofficial strike game, an art college game, even a game built round Marx's 18th Brumaire.

The projects I have described – which are only a handful from the many we have worked on in five years – seem, at first sight, to be very varied in content. But they have been built around a common philosophy – that people learn more quickly and eagerly and intensely from play situations than from formal subject teaching. And the projects have always had a common core of experience. We have tried to imagine and invent situations in which people would learn together; would bring their own individual skills to a collective purpose, and then push those skills to the limit; would discover other skills they never knew they possessed; would learn how to work at problems logically, and make discriminatory judgements; above all, would come to see themselves and their environment in a questioning, estranged way – and also to see possible ways of changing both.

Most of the work I have described has been done in an art college context. But its implications seem to me to be much wider. For the students I worked with, particularly in the early years at Bradford, were not either 'academic' in the conventional sense (many had no 'O' levels) or 'fine artists'. They were, for the most part, people who'd been regarded as failures at school, who'd come to a 'vocational' college, which didn't demand qualifications, and who regarded themselves as essentially practical people. Yet these students were soon staging a Russian Revolution in the streets, doing their own poetry readings in pubs, making plays and taking them to Amsterdam, and Zagreb, and Poland, running their own magazines, making their own radio tapes. Just as I, playing games while rehearsing

Ars Longa had discovered, after more than ten years as a teacher, ways of learning that I'd never imagined, so they, after barren, depressing years in secondary schools, were discovering that they, too, could produce work that was enjoyable on the highest level, and that other people would take seriously.

But why had they spent all these depressing years? And if they'd gone to a technical college to learn electrical wiring, instead of having come to an art college to learn textile design, wouldn't they have been condemned to go on with the depressing process? But, on the other hand, wouldn't it be possible to devise a way of teaching electrical wiring that would also be built around play – and would, therefore, extend, at the same time, the questioning, reasoning, and imaginative abilities of those students, too?

At the beginning of this chapter I wrote that it's generally agreed that young children learn through play – but that it's also agreed that adults don't. And the trouble is that we are all, successful and unsuccessful alike, conditioned in schools to accept that 'serious' learning must be formal, verbal, and fragmented into acceptable 'subjects.' So that play becomes marginal, and work, by definition, dull.

The work I've experienced over the last few years has been anything but dull. But it only became possible through a rejection of traditional concepts that separate 'work' from 'play'.

I've suggested that one of the aims of our work has been to encourage people to question themselves and their environment. And one of the aspects of that environment that most urgently needs questioning is an educational system that consigns enjoyment to the sports field – and play to young children.

BRIAN WINSTON

Self-help: the Media

The book is the earliest of modern mass communication systems. Books enable multiple transmissions of the same message to be made to large numbers of people. This *multiple* transmission aspect of typography is the essential characteristic which it shares with all other systems of mass communications. Further, some – McLuhan amongst them – would claim universal literacy and education are a function of typography. So books are not only a mass medium but also the corner stone of modern education. The learning process, whether undertaken informally by oneself or formally inside an educational institution, has depended on the book.

Education and books have become inextricably intertwined, but education has been less successful in absorbing the newer systems of mass communications. Indeed much of the cultural hostility to films, newsprint and both radio and television broadcasting comes from professional educators. These newer forms are deemed to threaten the book culture and so, at the same time, threaten education. But, however dangerous they are considered to be, they are nevertheless sources of information, and, as such, they have won a grudging place even in the book-dominated classroom. Schools, universities and institutions of adult education use a variety of media as audio-visual aids. The crucial word in this familiar phrase is the last – *aids*. The use of film strip or slide, live radio or television broadcasts, taped audio or audio-visual material, or film is seen essentially as an *aid* to traditional teaching. The educational system forces all these newer media into the pattern of the book – the first of such teaching aids. This ensures that their potential as educational tools is effectively limited. It is not surprising that this should be so since to fully exploit the educational potential of the new media would mean total disruption. After all the very architecture of educational institutions is determined by the book and the need to write. To substitute other media for the book would involve a different architecture and different teaching methods. Thus the newer media are allowed into the educational system as further sources of information but only in so far as they do not disrupt the nexus of book and class room.

We are now promised further advances in the distribution systems of the newer media. Each of these advances poses a further threat to the educational system. Each of these advances offers great possibilities for the growth of non-institutional informal education. In this they are not new. So far we have seen the system recast all threatening media in the form of the book and absorb them into the institutions. It is as likely as not that the system will similarly de-fuse these new advances.

The promised advances are in three main areas. Firstly, there will be an expansion of broadcasting using further bands in the electromagnetic spectrum. Secondly, cables will be used to carry radio and television signals. Cable capacity, unlike broadcasting, is not limited by natural bandwidth considerations. Consequently cables mean the possibility of an even greater proliferation of signals. Thirdly, systems will be introduced whereby film and videotape will be stored inside cassettes. In the case of film, the cassettes, many of which are already on the market, will dramatically reduce bulk and increase the ease with which they can be projected. Videotape will enable television material to be stored inside a cassette. These cassettes will be as small as paperbacks. They will be replayable on ordinary domestic television receivers and they will be no more complex to use than the currently available audio-cassettes or a long playing record — easier than the last, in fact.

Each of these developments has educational potential. With the expansion of broadcasting or cable *narrowcasting*, space could be made available for purely educational channels. The cassette development means that film and television for the first time can meet the book on equal terms. Cassettes are as portable as books and as easily operated as books. Most importantly the receiver will be able to turn to them at his or her own convenience. No longer will the receiver be tied to a specific time for a particular transmission. The transmission of the message will be controlled by the receiver as a reader controls the incoming information of a book. The cassettes could contain educational material as easily as entertainment matter.

For self-help in education the cassette development is the

most promising. To have available in one's home a series which demonstrates visually the techniques of a particular science or hobby obviously offers advantages over books dealing with the same topics. For a person interested in history, music or art the cassette will permit the transmission of greater and fuller, more vivid information than the book. The cassettes' capacity for replaying means that the watcher can dictate the speed at which he absorbs the cassettes' information. He can re-run sections of the film or tape which he failed to grasp at first playback – just as he can re-read a difficult page of text. The learning advantages offered by replay capacity are already being demonstrated in those schools which fully use audio cassettes. Children are given a language tape which they listen to by themselves. They control the speed at which they work through the tape. The film or TV cassette could be used in an identical way in schools. In the home audio-visual images could be slowed down, as it were, so that they yielded the maximum information.

All of this is not to herald the end of the book. Much information is still better contained inside books. The visualization of, say, philosophy is a difficult and in the final analysis thankless task. In fact, combinations of books and cassettes would seem best for a good many educational purposes. Perhaps more significantly, none of these developments, more broadcasting – cables – cassettes, means a revolution in communications, let alone in society.

There are a number of factors which should not be forgotten when trying to assess the societal effect of the introduction of new technology. More importantly, it should be remembered in this instance that we are talking about new distribution systems, not new media. It is of course possible that the replay capacity of the cassettes will alter the way material is presented on them. But, even if this happens, the viewer is still faced with a television screen. The informational capacity of that screen has not been altered merely because the signal it displays has been stored on narrowguage tape or film rather than received, via an aerial, from a transmitter. The technical history of the mass media shows how slow we are to absorb new media. For instance, Marconi's wireless was seen, as its name implies, as an alternative to wired telegraphy. That wireless could become a new medium, radio, was strangely ignored by the earliest pioneers.

In fact, for them the open quality of the signal they transmitted, that it could be picked up by any receiver, was a disadvantage when compared with the privacy of wired telegraphy or telephony.

Only sinking ships thought to broadcast – and, interestingly enough, the revolutionaries in Dublin during Easter 1916. For the first twenty years of the century wireless was allowed to plug the gaps in the wired system, mainly across oceans. The transmission of voices and music through the air, radio, was achieved by 1910 but radio stations were not introduced for another decade.

Two of the lines of development, extension of broadcasting and the introduction of cables, are analogous with the expansion of the wired telegraphy system and the introduction of wireless at the beginning of the century. Cables could mean the growth of community television services but such a growth is easily controlled by the power élite, as is broadcasting expansion. Neither of these developments need disrupt the existing media structures in any way.

The same is true, less obviously, of cassettes. If they are to yield new forms, as radio spun off from wireless telephony, we can expect a considerable time lag despite the enthusiasm of the manufacturers. It should not be forgotten that the driving impetus behind the cassettes is a commercial one. On the one hand there is a contracting entertainment industry with shelves and shelves of material which has now been exploited in cinemas and on television and which needs to be sold again. On the other hand there is the growth of the leisure market. For the manufacturers the gamble is obviously worth taking. Perhaps we shall indeed see people rushing to buy their own copies of *I Was a Teenage Werewolf* or *The Laugh-In,* both of which are promised as cassettes. More probable is that a market will exist for the sort of educational or leisure activity material referred to above. One can see the keen gardener usefully acquiring or hiring a *Percy Thrower* cassette or the historian his own copies of *The British Empire* series or the holiday maker a basic guide to Spain and Spanish.

Nevertheless all this latest development offers is a more convenient packaging of audio-visual information. All the material being offered is either already on film or could be transferred to film. The cassette players are about the same price as 16 mm sound film projectors. These days projectors are much simplified. The threat of video-cassette competition is making them easier still. But the point is that film is not widely used for either entertainment or educational purposes in the home, and it never has been. It is extraordinary then to place such reliance on the cassettes which are, by and large, films repackaged. Certainly film hiring costs are high but that is because few hire them. The cheapness of the cassettes is dependent on creating a mass market for them. The same could have happened with film but did not because films were shown in cinemas. Similarly, though, cassette material is broadcast on television. In fact, films in the home are used for only two purposes – home movies and pornography. Neither of these forms are available anywhere else. Cassettes are not being designed for either of these uses. The enthusiast can already hire, on film, the sort of educational or leisure material mentioned above. The BBC series *Civilization* is available. Educationalists will know the immense range of material on offer from specialized film libraries. Many of these libraries are now being transferred lock stock and barrel into cassettes. By all this one is not denying that in this new form they will be more easily, and perhaps more cheaply used. But one hestitates to ascribe to a packaging change the epithet *revolutionary*. Our enthusiasm for the potentially radical uses of cassettes and indeed of broadcasting expansion and cables must be tempered with an understanding of their essentially *one-way* bias.

All the systems of mass communication we have thus far invented have a one-way bias. They are centralized and hierarchic. This is no accident since, in this, they accurately reflect the essentially centralized hierarchic nature of our society. Thus all mass media are sources of information, not channels of communication. And the development promised are, similarly, sources like those already well established. These developments have potential as channels, as two-way systems. But this potential will be suppressed since it runs contrary to the fundamental bias of our communication systems. Indeed one could go so far as to suggest that the introduction of these new distribution systems is dependent on the suppression of their two way capability.

Looking at the various systems of cassettes being offered, one is struck by the fact that cameras and microphones, the machines needed to register the information onto the cassette, are often added to the system as an afterthought. Essentially the cassette devices are players not recorders. They are therefore a source device, not a channel. The manufacturers claim that their experience with audio-cassettes proves the public are more interested in buying pre-recorded material than in making their own. They judge the same will be true of video cassettes. They are not wrong. The one-way bias of communication systems has created a passive attitude towards the media. The professionals who work with the newer media encourage this passivity by insisting on mystifying the technicalities involved. With the older media the educational system makes sure that the majority learn enough to be able to consume but not to produce. Thus the whole consumerist tendency of our society encourages the receiver of messages to find it inconceivable that he could also become a transmitter. This factor, combined with the one-way bias of the systems themselves, means that these new developments will not automatically encourage self-help in education or any other field. People are not equipped to take over the community TV stations that the cables make possible. Nor is it likely they will want to. Similarly they will be more interested in buying *Percy Thrower* gardening cassettes than in sending him cassettes of their own gardening efforts. The cassette systems depend on a passive consumer. Their introduction seeks to create a new mass market. It is absurd to suggest that the consumer will have greater control over them simply because he can run them backwards and forwards. He has had such control over books for centuries but has never been encouraged to become a book producer. Therefore in this context self help can only be seen in terms of consumer patterns. Of themselves none of these developments are revolutionary.

What, then, are the prospects? There will certainly be an extension of the range of broadcasting. Recently an attempt by the existing commercial broadcasters in Britain to take over the fourth national channel for advertisements was defeated. This at least means that alternative structures can be considered for running this fourth channel. Perhaps it can be used wholly for education. But whatever form the fourth, and indeed the fifth and sixth, channels take they will be centralized and hierarchic.

The one-way bias of the media will not be altered by the use of these additional channels. Further the experience of the Open University has pointed up the difficulties involved in using a broadcasting channel for educational purposes. Open University broadcasts are seen as much as audio-visual aids as the projector in the school classroom. They are used to supplement the book teaching of the University. The University has established centres where the student can come face to face with an instructor. In other words, the Open University has very hesitantly tackled the problems involved in totally destroying the traditional notion of an educational institution. It has utilized media technology – books and broadcasting – to allow home study. But of the two the books seem to be the more important. If one listens to or watches an Open University broadcast one is impressed by how little it stands by itself. The references which place the broadcast into the pattern of study are incomprehensible to the outsider. In fact, where it not for the high cost of cassette players, all Open University broadcasts would obviously be better off on cassettes. So far the University has installed the newer film cassette players in the study centres only. They are too expensive to allow every student to own one. And anyway too much reliance on broadcasting is not a good thing. Broadcasts required attendance at a fixed time. Repeating the broadcasts only partially alleviates this problem. Broadcast transmit information at a fixed rate. However many times the broadcast is repeated it cannot be adjusted to suit the needs of each individual student. Videotape recording devices already help solve some of these problems in schools although, since the videotape recorder is as expensive as the cassette player, they cannot help the Open University student. In schools owning a videotape recorder, programmes can be recorded *off-air* and the resultant tape used as and when the schools particular timetable requires it. But air space is precious and this is an expensive method of distribution. It is a matter of concern that broadcasting in general does not reflect the full range of opinions in society nor does it cater for all tastes. Its tone is predominately middle-class. The justification for this narrowness is the limitation of bandwidths and therefore of time. In such a situation it seems pointless to extend a specialized use when that use can be better accommodated by videotape on reels or in cassettes. The spare broadcasting capacity should be used to increase the real balance of broadcasting output in general.

This objection does not apply to cables. They do not absorb precious air space and have such large channel capacities that they could and should be used for educational purposes. However, until they are widely in use, they do not help institutions like the Open University since the signal cannot be received outside a wired building. The prototype for the domestic cable development can be seen in the Local Education Authorities' or other educationalist institutions' use of closed circuit systems. These systems give the educationalist greater control over the material than with broadcasting. They enable the system to transmit programmes more conveniently. They also enable a certain amount of replying.

So far domestically the cables have only been used to carry ordinary broadcasting signals. The impetus behind the cables was the need in North America to increase the range of commercial choices available to the viewer and to improve the reception of local stations in heavily built up urban areas. Now the broadcasting regulatory agencies are beginning to insist that the cable operators also originate programmes on a community basis. The development in Great Britain has been slower. We are not faced with the same reception problems and there are no television signals that we cannot all, give or take a few underpopulated areas, receive. However some cable systems do already exist commercially and one has just been licensed to *narrowcast*. The sub-broadcasting standard video-tape equipment used in the educational closed circuit systems could also be used to establish community stations. These devices, of which the cassette players are a spin off, are comparatively cheap: £10,000 to £15,000 for the hardware to establish such a station would be a reasonable estimate. This compares more than favourably with broadcasting equipment costs, where £15,000 will not buy one camera, let alone a whole studio.

The crucial factor is that the cables do not require the same quality of signal as the transmission masts. Thus the cheaper equipment can be used and still produce satisfactory results in the home. All of this could matter a great deal. The cables offer the possibility of educational channels on Local Educational Authority or Open University lines. For a city wired with cable and reserving one channel for such a use the possibilities are great. Even institutes could reach right into the home. Programmes could be broadcast again and again for the convenience of the home student. Leaving aside the capital outlay of the cables themselves, such a service could be run extremely cheaply. And the wires could perhaps be paid for by commercial operations on the other channels. The cables offer great opportunities for community *narrowcasting* on a broader basis as well. Already in North America the cable cameras are invading town council meetings and the like. For the first time the technology offers a real chance to break down the one way bias and to allow television to become a two-way channel of communication. Of these possibilities, the former educational use which preserves the one-way bias and leaves the receiver as consumer, seems, if only for those reasons, to be the likelier.

The cassette situation is far more confused. The manufacturers, who have coined the phrase 'the cassette revolution', have so far been more successful in publicising their machines than in bringing them to the market. The Association of Cinematographic and Television Technicians, one of the British communication industries' unions, after careful study doubted whether the cassettes would actually make much impact on home entertainment for a decade or more. In this context entertainment includes leisure material. There are other problems. At the moment there is a plethora of systems either on the market or in the last stages of development. Firstly there are reel-to-reel recorders. These range in price from £200 to £10,000. They use tapes of various sizes to record the television image – $1''$, $\frac{2}{3}''$, $\frac{1}{2}''$ and $\frac{1}{4}''$. Where two manufacturers use the same tape size, the tapes are not compatible between them because they use different recording techniques. This applies to different machines in certain ranges manufactured by the same firm. Tapes recorded in North America are generally unplayable on European machines and vice-versa. Nevertheless thousands of machines have been sold mainly for educational and industrial training purposes. There is little pre-recorded material available for such machines, although there could be. Normally they are the heart of a production system which includes microphones, cameras, switching panels and display monitors. These last sometimes double as ordinary television receivers but these systems generally cannot play back into the domestic set. At their most advanced they could service the community or educational television stations.

The cassette players represent the next generation of the reel-to-reel machines. They do not need elaborate threading and can play into the domestic receiver. But here again there are a number of totally incompatible systems. In addition to different tape sizes, different recording systems and different standards of electricity there is the problem of different cassette designs. No manufacturer's cassettes will fit into any other manufacturer's player. Although cameras and microphones will be offered they are not the essence of the system. There are a number of cassette players available which use film and not videotape. These are not blighted by electronic incompatibilities but each manufacturer has designed his own unique cassette which, again, will not work in anybody else's projector. There are also more way-out devices using film as if it were tape or laser light. One manufacturer is going to sell videodiscs. Obviously not all these systems can succeed and at this stage it is impossible to say which one will win. But it is equally clear that the establishment of any sort of library of cassette material is going to beset by difficulties until a winner emerges. It would be a brave man who opted for one system over another at present and a very rich man who could afford the players for every system being offered.

The point remains that whatever their use for self-help in education none of these advances will mean any real change in the essential one-way bias of the media. They will all exhibit the same faults, distortions, half truths, and commercialisation that the established media exhibit. The only real chance of self-help in the media for educational or any other purpose will come when it is generally realized that these can be systems of two-way communication, not just sources of information. In among the devices mentioned above there are portable cassette recorders with attached cameras. They weigh only pounds, are battery powered, and the cameras are scarcely bigger than a man's hand. They are the best machines we have yet devised for capturing impressions of reality. Above all they are as simple to use as record-players. If inserted into the educational institutions not as teaching aids but as learning machines, they could enable young people to establish a familiarity with the audio-visual media which would destroy the one-way bias. That is to say a generation would grow up that understood the potential of all the media and could work them effectively. That is not say that every child would become a great television producer any more than every child now becomes a great writer. We can all write more or less (but, due to the efforts of the system, mainly less) and yet there are still professional writers. However there are no longer professional letter-writers amongst us. With all the media except print we are still at the professional letter-writing stage. Until we advance beyond this all media will match enlightenment with suppression. Each new advance will simply be used to exploit us further. In such circumstances the degree of self-help the new advances permit is illusory. We can only hope to help ourselves to an even greater passivity. We have lived in that relationship with the book and therefore with education for centuries. We have thus far failed to break the pattern with any of the newer media. Cables and cassettes are unlikely to break it for us.

RICHARD ROWSON

Learning for Learning's Sake

By learning for learning's sake, we generally mean study undertaken primarily for the intrinsic value and interest of the subject itself, and not as a means to something else – a good job, or enhanced social status. To demand that students, particularly working-class students, undertake study which will not result in any forseeable, tangible benefit, is to ask them to do something they are simply not inclined to do. This disinclination does not stem primarily from a lack of interest in anything not directly associated with tangible benefits, but from feelings and misconceptions about studying itself. Many people on the blue-collar ladder feel that learning for learning's sake is a luxury they have no time for, and that interest in certain areas – particularly the arts – is incompatible with being 'a worker', since it is part of the trappings of being 'middle-class'. Once these feelings are overcome, and once a student is no longer made to feel *obliged* to take up this sort of interest, his inclination towards, and capacity for, learning for learning's sake can surprise even himself.

The major factors contributing to students' misconceptions about study for its own sake are rooted in educational institutions themselves. There is the obvious attitude, adopted by many of them, that studying is a process of absorbing as much information as possible for regurgitation in exams: the more exams passed, the more successful the 'education' is judged. The sad thing is that the schools whose reputation is often the highest in any community are those which appear to hold this attitude most strongly. Equally obvious is the inference to be drawn from this attitude – that if you do not want, or cannot attain, whatever it is that results from passing exams, then there is no purpose in studying.

A similar attitude is that studying is a matter of competing with other people. Competition is often first used as an incentive to study, but becomes so integrated into the studying system that, for most people, the two become indistinguishable. The

113

competitive attitude results in the students' attention becoming focused on completing *prescribed* work, and on comparing his performance in it with that of others, rather than in considering the value intrinsic to his performance. The more competent he is at study, the greater the pressures for him to do this, and the less chance he has to reflect, to follow his own interests, or to make spontaneous explorations. To many people it must seem that the better you are at study, the less it is related to you as an individual, the more tension-ridden it becomes, and the more it demands total conformity from its participants. Such people are therefore unlikely to regard study as something to be voluntarily undertaken, or as a process which can have anything to do with their individual, spontaneous interests, or as potentially enriching to them as individuals. Study, with its competitive associations, is likely to seem totally alien to any inclinations they may have to develop their own interests, at their own pace.

There is also that view of studying which reduces it merely to a process of memorising and being able to reproduce facts and opinions. Status-seeking is responsible for this, as well as the attitudes of the institutions: if you can remember lots of things and reiterate them, you can impress people, you can feel secure that you know *something*. But learning for learning's sake is not concerned with this.

If study is not just the amassing of information, nor is it that other misconceived extreme, an entrée into the world of higher mysteries, such that, when asked to explain what he does, the practitioner is entitled to smile enigmatically and by his attitude suggest that no explanation is possible, except to the initiated. Admittedly it is not easy instantly to explain many areas of learning, not because they are mysterious and elevated realms inaccessible to the common herd, but because they are extremely complex. The lack of mystery, but great complexity, of many branches of learning is often not brought out by their teachers, who would often rather not run the risk of boring – and disillusioning – their students by lengthy and sometimes pedestrian analyses of a particular problem, which analyses might locate the place where difficulty and confusion lie. Instead, these teachers prefer oblique approaches, and allusions to complexities too knotty to unravel. Consequently learners are not given the chance to become familiar with, and competent at handling, the most profound ideas of their subject: the process is not properly designed to impart them. Yet gaining such an understanding of, and familiarity with, the conceptual scheme of a subject, and learning how to handle and work with its basic ideas, are vital parts of study. I have several times met students for their first tutorials in philosophy when their only contact with the subject has been a reading of some elusive introduction to it. They have arrived, not with a burning desire to clear up some of the mysteries, but with a hostile attitude, angry at having spent a long time puzzling over abstract and unfamiliar ideas, only to find their efforts led nowhere. Several tutorials have begun by my being told that philosophy is airy-fairy nonsense. Many students' sole motivation for attending the tutorials has been to obtain the angry satisfaction of provoking or witnessing such confrontations.

I do not draw attention to these institutionally-produced factors to make yet another pious statement that institutions must change their ways, but to make more people aware that much of any jaundiced view they may hold of study arises from their experience of institutions, and is not a reflection of what study can be. I have met many people who have taken up learning for its own sake as a free and voluntary activity, who have found it a far more rewarding and involving activity than they remember study as being. They remember it as something which they undertook, willingly or unwillingly, when they were younger, and when they were so bombarded with possibilities of immediate change and development on so many levels in their lives that the impact of intellectual ideas faced too strong competition to be felt deeply, or given the consideration it deserved. Later, when the practical pattern of their lives has become established, they have felt the need for intellectual stimulation, and have been more open to it. I find that such older students generally have a greater relish for ideas, are more involved in their study, and often, as a result, progress more quickly than younger students whose work is part of an institutionally prescribed scheme.

There were excellent examples of this at the Summer Schools held by the Open University in 1971. The University operates through a type of correspondence course, linked to radio and television programmes and (approximately) weekly discussions, or lectures held in study centres throughout the United Kingdom. Halfway through their first year of study, students attended a one-week Summer School. Their ages ranged from twenty-one to over eighty, and their educational backgrounds were equally varied. For all of them, the philosophy content of their study was a case of learning for learning's sake, and at the Summer School they spent five hours in groups of about fifteen students per tutor – a totally new experience for them – discussing a problem of philosophy which was also new to them. They had earlier only read and done some exercises in Cartesian philosophy and logic.

The philosphy tutors were mostly full-time lecturers at other universities, and they were amazed at the general level of discussion, argument and writing in the tutorials, and the degree of involvement and philosphical sophistication reached by the students. It was higher than they would have expected to reach with many first-year full-time students after two terms. Tutors were required to go far more deeply into the philosophical problems than they anticipated, and they received much more back from the students in the form of spontaneous counter-arguments and newly thought-out ways of approaching the problem than from first-year undergraduates.

But all this is not limited to those who take up philosophy. Most part-time tutors (and there are several hundred) of the Open University, who are concerned with science, the social sciences, mathematics, the arts, do not regard the payment as their main incentive to taking these posts, but the opportunity to work with students who are highly motivated. Tutors do not have to spend time and energy stimulating these students. They feel that for once their skills are being fully used, that they are dealing with people who take full advantage of the benefits to be gained, and who are stimulating and valuable to teach.

The feelings of freedom, self-assertion, and satisfaction which come from studying what you want to study are powerful incentives to overcoming difficulties which dog students not motivated in the same way. Institutions should not *demand* of students that they learn for learning's sake. Their only role, if they have one at all, should be to make people aware of the facilities they can offer to anyone wishing to study.

When someone has an interest he wishes to pursue, he may be able to find out about it from his library – where, if he is not himself adept at manipulating the system, he can obtain help from the librarians. Ideally, through the library he should be able to obtain all types of audio-visual material, and be able to consult a catalogue of interests containing the names and addresses of people sharing those interests in his locality. Two-way communication with others about a subject makes studying it more valuable. At present the student is likely to find in his library, at least in Britain, a list of clubs and perhaps individuals interested in photography, archaeology, and amateur dramatics, but not one for studies which are more abstract. This is not because libraries refuse to list such interests, as though they were pornographic, but because people do not volunteer the information. As it is, the student should search through the lists of local education authorities, groups, and universities, or even advertise in the local paper for people with similar interests. Through these channels he may be able to join discussion groups or attend weekend or full-week courses for like-minded students. These are usually stimulating events, but the student should also try to find one or two people whose judgements in the field he respects, and who are prepared to give detailed attention to his ideas, and appraise them with him.

He may be able to find local teachers in schools or universities who are prepared to see him informally. Most people, however, are only likely to obtain access to someone willing and able to discuss their subject if they first register as students in an educational institution, and regularly attend a prescribed course of study there. The student would be well-advised, failing all else, to do this. The course may serve his interest admirably, and even if it does not he may find people attending or running the course with whom he can have separate discussions. But ideally the student should be able first to see, privately, someone informed and able to discuss his interests at length, and only in the light of these discussions should the student consider attending a relevant course.

If the student is unable to find anyone whom he can acknowledge as fulfilling a tutorial role towards him, he should try to find someone with whom he can talk or to whom he can write

117

on a more or less equal basis. Such a person can perform at least some of the functions of a tutor.

The tutor's first job is to encourage his student to put his understanding of and reaction to what he has read into words. This often clarifies matters, and can provide a basis for discussion. It is easy to read a complex sentence with a mistaken emphasis, or to expect that something is going to be said and so read it into a sentence when it isn't there. If alone, one can read and reread endlessly without discovering the source of one's confusion. A student once come to me in misery, after spending a week trying to understand a logical problem. He realized his mistake in just ten seconds. As I read the problem though, he saw that he'd inserted an imaginary comma in his reading, so altering the sense.

The tutor may also suggest difficulties about the ideas, or ask questions which may not have occurred to the student; and help him to relate these ideas to others, or see them in a different context, or to apply them to different problems. The tutor may also relieve the pressures of new ideas on the student, by which I mean the situation in which a student is overwhelmed by ideas that are totally novel to him. By discussing them with someone else, especially someone able to argue about them and their limitations, the students can be helped to distance himself from the ideas, and to see them in perspective. The disturbing effect of new ideas on people – particularly adults – studying voluntarily, alone, and exposed to such ideas for the first time, is often under-estimated by teachers in institutions. These teachers have usually long grown accustomed to the ideas they handle; their students are often not as highly motivated as people learning voluntarily for learning's sake, and are therefore less sensitive to the ideas put before them, besides having plenty of opportunity to discuss them with fellow-students and staff.

There are also times in the situation of voluntary learning for its own sake when a tutor has to take a firm line with the student, to question (as well as advise on) the methods he has adopted, and to stretch and test the student's skill in operating the techniques of the subject matter. In philosophy, this would involve testing the logic of the student's arguments, *not* testing him to see how much of other people's arguments he had remembered, or adopted. Occasionally the tutor might ask the student to do what he doesn't want to do – he may feel the need to widen the learner's interests, which may mean going against the learner's motivation for a time. But if he does so, he must always be able to justify his request to the student. If the student does *only* what he is most strongly motivated to do, he may not be as thorough or as comprehensive in his study as he needs to be to gain a clear understanding of the subject.

In putting forward the need by students for the help of others, I am not suggesting that they are inadequate in any way. The most seasoned and professional handlers of ideas usually do not commit themselves to their views until they have thoroughly tested them against the reactions of people they respect. What I am suggesting is that most people, at least until they are over the initial stages of becoming familiar with an area of study, can benefit from communicating – ideally by the tutorial method – with someone more familiar with that area. I am not suggesting that the student should not question his tutor's methods and advice: for the most part, the sooner he feels able to do this, the more stimulating he will find it. If his tutor does not consider the student's viewpoint, or does not seem to give a fair appraisal of his case, then the student should try to find someone else to appraise it. If everyone he finds appraises it critically, then he should have the humility to reconsider it, although always relying on his own judgement, and not necessarily assuming it is he who is mistaken.

I began by claiming that learning for learning's sake is something that must begin with the student's own motivation, not with any institutional pressures, and I have emphasized the desirability of learning being shaped and directed by the student's individual interests (although with the help of a tutor), not by institutional prescriptions.

In principle I do not see why this tutorial activity should not take place without any school or college system as we now know it (provided a register was kept of people in a locality pusuing particular interests), or why people should not select their tutors on the basis of personal suitability, rather than by relying on some official certification of tutors. Certainly in philosphy it is important for the success of the student-tutor relationship that the student should try to get a tutor whom he respects, yet whom he feels confident in questioning; whom the

the student can clearly understand, or question until he understands, and whom he trusts to understand him. The establishment of such a relationship is more important than trying to get the tutor with the highest certificated qualifications available.

No doubt, in an ideal world, people would take on tutorial responsibilities for the simple love of their interest. In practice, however, they would need to be paid for the time they were occupied as tutors – particularly if they were popular ones. But if they were paid for their hours of teaching only, whether by the students or by some other source, then their living would be precarious – subject to fashion, even – and they would not have the security necessary to further their own study thoroughly. I cannot see how some branches of learning could survive in a vital form without people being in some way guaranteed a livelihood to follow their interests in them, irrespective of personal popularity or success as a tutor. It therefore seems to me inevitable that in any practical system there would be recognized scholars who, though they may not necessarily be certificated as such, would represent an 'establishment' in that branch of learning, and attract students on this basis alone, regardless of tutorial prowess. Reputation amongst students alone would seem an impractical basis on which a learner could begin to select a tutor. There might need to be some system of 'recognizing' tutors, though based rather on their ability as tutors than on their having undergone prescribed courses of study in educational institutions.

Although students and tutors could meet without any need for an educational institution, for many areas of study they would need access to equipment which might need to be shared on an organized basis. There would also need to be some system whereby tutors could discuss and pursue their own learning but, again, this could be set up without any need for teaching institutions.

The practical difficulties in organizing communications between students and tutors on a voluntary and at least partially individual basis are not easily solved. They would demand, at the least, a reorganization of educational priorities and a redistribution of educational effort. But the demand for tutors and equipment would perhaps be no greater afterwards than it is now. More important, the tutors and teachers, instead of spending a large part of their efforts in trying to stimulate interest in their subject, would find themselves dealing with people already interested in learning – a situation most would find idyllic.

Learning for learning's sake is more a matter of acquiring skills than of gathering information : becoming familiar with the material of a subject by handling it, by learning how to use it. Inevitably, in many areas of study, the student must spend time taking in information about other people's ideas, proofs, and techniques. But he should do so actively – questioning them, doing exercises with them, working out their implications, thinking whether he can improve them. In this he needs the help of other people. As his familiarity with the material grows, he can become more adventurous in the way he handles it: he can start his own projects once he has some criteria by which to judge his own performance. It must be emphasized that studying is a vital, natural affair – in fact, it is how we learn to do anything we particularly want to do.

Learning in the sense of 'study' is, or should be, more a process of 'learning how' than 'learning what'. If it were more commonly regarded as being a 'learning how' activity, then learning for learning's sake would seem and would be a relevant, acceptable, and valuable activity.

JOE RAVETZ

Learning Without Schools: a Pupil's View

This essay intends to give some 'inside' information on various practical means of education outside of schools, based on my own experiences. The 'deschooler' here is not someone who follows the very sophisticated philosophies of writers such as Ivan Illich. He is rather a person who is disillusioned and alienated by the school scene, but who wants to continue his 'education', and so intentionally leaves school after the minimum age. However, he (or she; throughout 'he' will stand for 'he or she') will not automatically enrol in the nearest college; he will consider the acquisition of learning in an active sense, experimenting with different forms of education, and accepting no absolute authorities above him. He will approach education from the side of the liberal tradition rather than the exam-oriented slant of the courses that he will actually encounter.

I use 'education' here in a dual sense: the traditional meaning of passing exams as a means to continuing 'education' at a higher level, and finally to getting a well paid job; and also the more progressive sense of being in contact with academic subjects in a spontaneous and creative way, as one part of being in contact with 'life' and 'reality' in general. It is this dual course that a practical education must take *at the present time*; for, however much the progressives may theorize, exam qualifications still function as the traditional salary-doubler. A good practical education will strike the mean between these two opposing qualities, the desirable and the necessary.

Case history of a deschooler

My background was in an English middle-class, liberal-progressive university home. When I was eight the local primary school was getting too much for me, so I changed to the nearest direct-grant grammar school. This was satisfactory for the next six years, but in the fifth form, the O-level year, new troubles arose. Simultaneously the teaching grew more boring, while the teachers and the headmaster increasingly resented and repressed individuality, and I and some friends were growing more restless and insubordinate. After several incidents and confrontations I obtained an educational psychiatrist's certificate to stay off school for most of the Lent term, which I then did. At Easter I decided, with my parents, to leave school, coming in again only for the exams, and so all through the summer term I wasted no time at school, but worked, quite successfully, on my own at home. After the exams I left quietly, with much hand-washing on the part of the masters.

In the autumn I signed on for two courses at the local College of Further Education (CFE) in art and history; also an 'introductory' physics course at the university, music with a private teacher, and mathematics with a university friend of my father's. I worked very hard for the first few weeks, and then slackened off to a very low level for the rest of the term, an action which I am still regretting. In a few weeks I dropped the art course, which I felt was not teaching me anything new. After a term I suspended the maths lessons: I was discouraged because the teacher had actually overestimated my ability, a thing which is generally very rare for teachers to do. I changed the CFE history, which was simply boring, to regular private discussions with a student friend; but these were only temporary, and anyway I was not very interested in history at that time.

My intention is to get to university, so for my own good I need the exam results; so the present situation is an uneasy compromise between doing academic work and my own work, artistic and political. The depressing compromise between the good and the necessary easily arises in this fashion.

Problems of deschooling

There are three main problems that the prospective practical deschooler faces. The first is the actual decision; the next and the most concrete one is the choosing of courses in various places in accordance with certain limits and factors; the last and most difficult problem is to allot time efficiently and to keep up work and morale.

The initial decision is obviously going to be undertaken for a variety of reasons. Many people have to leave school because of age, or financial reasons, before they have passed their set of exams satisfactorily. These people usually gravitate towards the local CFE to study for exams and re-takes on a part-time basis; this is how the colleges get the reputation of being cram-factories. Other people are expelled from school, often for political reasons, and they go various ways, one of which can be the freelance way I am describing.

For the intentional deschooler, the reasons are well-known and widely spread. You may be bored and frustrated with the school structure and routine; you may be unable to do the subjects you want, or to get good enough teaching to satisfy you; you may be tired of the people at school and want to find new circles; you may have personal conflicts with the authorities above, so that they will eventually give you a bad report for university. Any one of these reasons, or (as in my case) a combination of them all can be enough to make your decision. Your attitude is usually summed up by the clumsy phrase 'he doesn't like school', or 'school doesn't turn him on' (not that I have ever heard of school turning anybody on). If school quite definitely does not turn you on, and if you are old enough, there is nothing legal to stop you leaving. But to do so profitably requires the working out of numerous problems, especially if you have long-term goals in mind, such as higher education.

It does help a lot to have sympathetic parents. I was aided enormously by my parents who were both sympathetic, had contacts, and the spare money to use them. Parents can aid you in many other ways, not least of which is general moral support. This might be swayed your way by well-placed casual remarks in conversations. If they are completely opposed, you can try and convince them with all the rational arguments of the progressive educational philosophers; if that fails, which is likely, all that you can do is to be blunt and say that you simply refuse to go back to the school next term, and that you have made other arrangements. They should recognize that you have your own problems of adolescence, and that in a school these would be suppressed so that you would grow up mentally much less healthy. If you are of school-leaving age, your parents are likely

124

to still have economic power over you; but they should not have the moral tyranny to apply economic power without consultation on your interest.

Choosing of methods

On the choosing of various courses in various places, the factors which determine your choice are as follows: academic and social desirability of institutions, with subjects offered and qualifications for entry; money, geographical position; and obligations involved. If you are aiming for A-levels or some other specific exam it is not always essential to take a course which is designed for that exam in particular. It is advisable to stick to the level that you need, but as long as you can pick up the basic material it is easy to adapt a course to your own special needs, if you write off for and study past papers and syllabuses first.

The institution which is officially designed to cater for the school-leaver who is continuing his education is the College of Further Education. These are usually very mixed up places, socially fragmented. It is true that the people expelled from school, who are likely to be interesting individuals, gravitate there, but they do so solely for the sake of exams. The colleges are run by the local authority, which might mean that they may may have no socializing facilities such as coffee bars; and many other types of people go there, such as nuns, policemen, and middle-aged middle-class housewives. There are no qualifications needed, and there is a minimum age of 16, but this is flexible.

The teaching in a college is not likely to be hopelessly incompetent, but neither is it likely to be brilliant and inspiring. Facilities and equipment, especially in the practical sciences and arts can vary from the very new and lavish to the very old and broken down. Generally, CFEs are satisfactory for cheap exam-passing, but not at all good for the combination of that with a liberal education, that the deschooler will be looking for.

There are numerous other types of colleges provided by the Local Education Authority, such as art colleges, music colleges, technical college, colleges of education, sixth form colleges, and the polytechnics. Most of these are mainly 'vocational' colleges for people who want to do fulltime courses for professional diplomas and certificates. Some of them will provide ordinary subjects as well, but these will be 'additional' courses for the people there already. With the possible exception of the sixth form colleges, most of them do not encourage ordinary people coming in for part-time lessons, and in fact the smaller ones tend to be rather insular. Some may provide 'recreational' classes in the evenings.

Some towns, however, provide institutes or centres for partly recreational, partly vocational subjects like art and music. Part-time courses, both non-exam and for GCE, are encouraged, and since the whole institution is devoted to the one subject, they can be quite effective. These institutions are linked, or similar to, the numerous Adult Educational Centres, which are mainly branches of the Workers' Educational Association or the extra-mural departments of universities. There are no strict age limits or entry qualifications, since, being essentially places for ordinary people to improve themselves, they do not run courses for exams at all. The teaching is usually very good; since there is no definite commitment and exam at the end of the course, it has to be in order to keep up attendances. The people who go there are not necessarily young and freaked-out, and the social scene sometimes assumes a kind of bourgeois part-time amateur-ish air, which probably does not suit most deschoolers rejoicing in their hairy youth.

Universities run one year 'remedial' and 'introductory' courses for many subjects, and provided you can get permission from the head of department you might be able to enrol as an occasional student. Arts subjects and social sciences would probably be very hard to get into, whereas science subjects would be quite easy. The teaching is likely to be good, and the company more alive than dead (which is sometimes not the case in CFEs, in my experience). But large civic universities, even with strong Unions, are traditionally very lonely places at first, and are even more so when you have no department to belong to. The local Education Office will supply detailed information on the colleges, but not on the university which is quite separate.

Institutions in general are useful for making social contacts and getting some sort of an education fairly cheaply. Other methods can be very much better for getting into the subjects themselves, but they are often lonely and inwardly directed in social effect, and they also cost a lot of money. Correspondence courses from places such as Wolsey Hall, Oxford, are good for making sure of exam passes; they present the syllabus in such a way that you do not unnecessary work at all. But I have been told that with some self-discipline, GCE tests cards and revision notes, together with 'Teach Yourself' books, can work just as well. The Open University would be good for the opposite extreme, a wide liberal educaton, but there is a strict lower age limit of 21.

Private tuition can often be the best method of learning, even if it is for only an hour a week. Getting a friend to help you and teach you is useful for some stimulation and inspiration, but being a friendly informal arrangement it tends to be rather temporary; in fact, the better the friend, the shorter the duration. Formal private tuition can fail for two reasons; personal antipathy or antagonism, or failure to keep up with the work either by the teacher or by the pupil. If you see these situations arising, then stop at once before your money and friendship is wasted. Music is the subject where private tuition is widely practised. Teachers for other subjects are usually university people or schoolteachers doing it on the side for a bit of extra money, and their quality can only be found by experiment. Possibly the ideal teaching situation is a kind of group tutorial where you sit round with some friends who are all very interested, and absorb the wisdom of the teacher; unfortunately these would be almost impossible to get together outside of a university, where something approaching this is done for you.

On the choosing of institutions generally, small or obscure institutions, or teachers who are 'interesting characters', are worth trying because they may be just what you want; but it is very important not to commit yourself before you have found out. It is often advisable to start with one or two courses more than you need, so that after a few weeks you can reject the ones which appeal to you the least. Always try to ask people who know the teacher before committing yourself. Once you have enrolled for your course, it is important to organize yourself quickly before enthusiasm slackens; this means doing things like getting set books, arranging a proper work place, and writing off for syllabuses and past exam papers. In the first few weeks it is a good idea to work quite hard: the teacher will expect more of you, and you will find out more about the course, which you might want to change before it is too late. It is an administrative bother to change in mid-year, but it is worth doing if you are not satisfied. And once you have started, it is always worth changing and experimenting to find the best arrangement.

Money and other factors

Money is the great problem in securing an education which is something more than a grind in the local CFE. I was helped enormously by my parents who had both the spare money and the willingness to spend it where I needed it.

The normal system for most LEA colleges is that if you are under 19, and if you attend full-time in one particular institution, it is free, or only for a small charge; if you are part-time in each of several institutions then you pay the part-time rate for each class, which is usually less than £10 a year, and is the same for everybody. If you are over 19, however, the full-time rate can be more than £50 a year, and if you are 'overseas', full-time will cost you the economic rate, more than £100 a year. Union fees are automatically levied, but they are not very much.

Adult Education centres, being subsidized by the LEA, cost less than £5 a year, and so do Music Institutes and similar places. Registration as an occasional student at a university can cost £30 with union fees, and the LEA will not subsidize you for that. One hour of private tuition a week, at £1.50, might cost £60 a year, although if it is with a friend it will cost nothing. Correspondence courses are generally in the same range as private tuition; revision notes are less than 50p. Public exams such as A-levels also cost about £4 each, which comes to a lot for a whole set; but if you are hard up the LEA should, with some pressure, give you something towards that.

If your parents can afford perhaps £50 a year for your betterment, then you should be able to persuade them to do so. If they cannot, then for the LEA institutions you should be able to get a grant, again with some pressure. If you find that family life turns you on even less than school, then if you are over 16 there is nothing legal to stop you leaving home. You could not then indulge yourself in a complete full-time education, for then you would not be able to get a dole to keep body and soul together. Your parents would be unlikely to pay the rent for you, and working at the same time as learning is too much hard work for anyone in this modern age.

Geographical position is useful to consider when choosing places dotted all over urban complexes. The more travelling time needed to and from a place, the more likely that your attendance will slacken off, especially in the winter months. If you live in a suburb then be wary of arranging things so conveniently that you never have to travel through the town: it is very easy to get lonely and isolated from the city. If possible, arrange lesson times on a few days a week; this saves travelling time and money, enables you to go for drinks between lessons, and enables you to work more intensively on the other days of the week.

The obligations involved in a course affect to a very large extent the efficiency of the course, and your general state of mind and morale. If no obligations are attached, you have paid no fees, there is no special exam, the teacher leaves you to work at your own pace, then the surfeit of freedom can ruin the course. On the other hand, if the obligations are too heavy, if you had to talk your way in without the proper qualfications, or if you like the teacher but he expects too much of you, then this can be very depressing. Obviously the golden mean has to be found and chosen.

Freedom and responsibility

Freedom, as any serious anarchist can tell you, puts infinitely more responsibility on a person than do laws and routines. In a way, when you deschool yourself, you are putting the anarchist ideal into practice; for the essential element of practical deschooling is that you are governed by nobody but yourself, that you are an inmate of no institution and have to comply with no rules and accept no misguidance, except those enforced by society itself. This position has as many disadvantages as advantages.

Government and authority first arose because they were *convenient*. A higher authority would arbitrate disputes, lead the people and act as a day-to-day moral guide, basically because otherwise everybody had to *think for themselves all the time*. Doing this is a very marvellous thing and in the end it will make us all a lot more civilized, but it puts an enormous strain on the person, both mental and moral. The very high suicide rate among artists in modern times is due largely to the freedom that they enjoy.

After ten or more continuous years at school, where lives are ordered and controlled in patterns that usually contain at least some vestige of efficiency, it is quite a shock to be suddenly confronted with this freedom. What normally happens, in fact, to the practical deschooler is that he does not 'live up to his own responsibility', but does no work until he realizes that he is messing himself up for the future, and then comes to terms with his freedom. This is what happens to many university students who have just left school; it happened to me as well, creating continuous depressions and friction with my family and friends.

It surprised and annoyed me that my old friends still in school seemed to have much more spare time than I did, in spite of all the time-wasting routines at school – prayers, compulsory games, and so on. But when you reject the misguidance and the paternalism of authority you also lose the guidance, organization and slight stimuli that are its advantages; it would be marvellous to have it both ways but that is virtually impossible to obtain. On your own, freelancing, much more time is spent organizing yourself, learning how to organize yourself, and discovering ways of educating yourself (for the real task of the ideal teacher is to teach the pupil to teach himself; no-one can do his learning for him). Sorting out the bureaucratic messes that you have created with your unorthodoxy also takes an appreciable amount of time, as do other things like increased travelling time, and experiments with different courses. Mismanagement of time can be one of the major reasons for failure of the deschooling programme.

To sum up: first decide, from your experience and this article, whether you want to continue your education in or out of a school. Then get all the available information from Education Offices and others, work out and *write down* a list of alternatives (timetable clashes can usually be avoided by writing off for the previous year's timetables). Meanwhile propagandize your parents and check them out on financial aid, then present them with the scheme that you have worked out. When you have reached a compromise, then enrol at the various places and organize yourself. Be prepared for anything that may come, such as freak-outs, depressions and loneliness: all these states are intensified without the mediating influence of a closed institution. The one thing that you are not likely to experience, however, is boredom: the road to freedom may not be easy, but it is always interesting.

Notes on Contributors

MICHAEL ARMSTRONG taught at Wandsworth before working at the Institute of Community Studies on the Leicestershire Plan for education, after which he joined the Nuffield Foundation's project Resources for Learning. He was a founder member of the Comprehensive Schools Committee, and its chairman from 1966 to 1971. Since 1970 he has been head of the social studies department at Leicester's Countesthorpe Community College.

PETER BUCKMAN read history at Balliol College, Oxford, before joining the editorial board of Penguin Books. He spent a year as editor with the New American Library, New York, before starting to write full time. He has published articles for journals varying from *OZ* to *The Times*, and is the author of *The Limits of Protest* and *Playground*, a game of fiction. He is married, with one daughter, and lives in Oxfordshire.

KEN COATES was born in 1930 and spent eight years down the mines of Nottinghamshire and Derbyshire before going to the University of Nottingham for a degree in sociology. He helped found the Institute for Workers' Control, and since 1960 has been teaching sociology at Nottingham University's Department of Adult Education. He has written extensively on poverty, education, and workers' control.

JOHN HIPKIN is a graduate of the London School of Economics and has taught in most kinds of British schools. He was senior research associate at the Centre for Applied Research in Education at the University of East Anglia, where he worked with Lawrence Stenhouse on the Humanities Curriculum Project. He has published a play, *The Massacre of Peterloo*, and co-edited a report of a Cambridge Union Teach-in *Education for the Seventies*. He is married with three children, and lives in Cambridge.

ALBERT HUNT is Senior Lecturer at the Regional College of Art, Bradford, where he directs the College Theatre Group, which has appeared all over Europe, twice winning awards at the Zagreb International Festival, most recently for *John Ford's Cuban Missile Crisis*. Albert Hunt collaborated with Peter Brook on the production of *US*, and is theatre critic of *New Society*.

IVAN ILLICH was born in Vienna in 1926 and went to America in 1951, where he served as assistant pastor in an Irish-Puerto Rican parish in New York City. From 1956 to 1960 he was assigned as vice-rector to the Catholic University of Puerto Rico. He was a co-founder of the Center for Intercultural Documentation (CIDOC) in Cuernavaca, Mexico, and since 1964 has directed research seminars on 'Institutional Alternatives in a Technological Society', with special focus on Latin America. He is the author of *Celebration of Awareness* and *Deschooling Society*.

IAN LISTER is at present Lecturer in Education at the University of York. He has written about deschooling and alternatives in education in the *Times Educational Supplement* and *Times Higher Educational Supplement*, and has presented papers on related topics to various European seminars. He is the Editor of *General Education*, and started an Open Seminar on reform in education at the University of York in the autumn of 1971.

MICHAEL MACDONALD-ROSS started as a biologist, and taught zoology and genetics at the University of London. He became interested in the application of the behavioural sciences to the problems of education, and joined the programmed learning organization Educational Systems Ltd, where he was Program Manager. Later he founded Instructional Systems Associates, an independent educational consultancy. He helped in the initial design of the Open University, and is now Senior Lecturer in the University's Institute of Educational Technology. He is 33 and married.

JOE RAVETZ was born in 1956 and attended state primary schools before going to grammar school at the age of eight. Having passed his GCE 'O' Levels he left school in order to study without the hindrances of an institution. He is now a prospective artist and writer earning his future living by working his way up the educational ladder. He would be glad to hear of others who have had experiences of school similar to his own.

RICHARD ROWSON was born in 1942 and schooled at the village primary school, where his father was headmaster, and at county grammar schools. He read philosophy at King's College, London, before doing social work for three years. He then ran optional courses in philosophy at a Technical College and Polytechnic, and took part in experimental day-courses of the National Extension College. He now works for the Open University, writing and researching courses in moral philosophy and education.

ALISON TRUEFITT and PETER NEWELL both worked as educational journalists: Alison Truefitt on the London *Evening Standard* and Peter Newell on the *Times Educational Supplement*, which he left to become Education Officer of the Cobden Trust, arm of the National Council for Civil Liberties. He and Alison Truefitt are working to set up an alternative school and community project in a poor part of London.

COLIN WARD is Education Officer for the Town and Country Planning Association, and edits their bulletin of environmental education *Bee*. He worked on housing and schools for several architectural firms before lecturing on liberal studies at Wandsworth Technical College. He was one of the editors of *Freedom* from 1947 to 1960, and the editor of *Anarchy* from 1961 to 1970. He is the author of two books in the Penguin Connexions series for schools, and is editing a book on vandalism for the Architectural Press.

BRIAN WINSTON attended Kilburn Grammar School and Merton College, Oxford, before spending eight years as a television producer with the BBC, and Granada, where he worked on *World in Action*. He is currently Director of Mass Communications Studies at Alvescot College in Oxfordshire, a branch of the State University of New York. He is working on a general background guide to the Media.